No Cost Jesus?

No Cost Jesus?

What Did Jesus Mean When He Said to Take Up Your Cross?

H. WALLACE WEBSTER

RESOURCE *Publications* · Eugene, Oregon

NO COST JESUS?
What Did Jesus Mean When He Said to Take Up Your Cross?

Resource Publications
An Imprint of Wipf and Stock Publishers
199 W. 8th Ave., Suite 3
Eugene, OR 97401

www.wipfandstock.com

PAPERBACK ISBN: 978-1-6667-0481-5
HARDCOVER ISBN: 978-1-6667-0482-2
EBOOK ISBN: 978-1-6667-0483-9

All Scripture quotations, unless otherwise noted, are from The Holy Bible: Containing the Old and New Testaments, New King James Version. Nashville: Nelson Bibles, 2006.

Quotations marked ESV are from *The English Standard Version Bible*. New York: Oxford University Press, 2009.

07/07/21

Contents

Acknowledgments

THERE ARE SO MANY people in my life that have lived this book in front of me. Obviously, there are too many to list completely. However, I do want to highlight a few of them that probably made the most lasting impact on my life.

First, I would like to dedicate this in the memory of my grandparents, Horace and Irene Webster. My "Pop" may actually have been my best friend growing up. He took me places and taught me how to crab, fish, and duck hunt. He will always stand out as one of my heroes. My "Mom" was one of those people that never seemed to sin. Of course, we know better theologically. But she truly lived a selfless and crucified life. She spent hours in the Word and on her knees. I believe I am today serving the Lord due to much of her consistent prayer life.

Second, I dedicate it in the memory of my parents, David and Nora Webster. They sacrificed their lives for me to have a great childhood and a chance to make a life for myself. They always pointed me to Jesus and lived it out loud daily. They never complained. They rarely bought things for themselves. As I look back, I can now see how they truly died to self and served. I will be forever grateful.

Lastly, I want to dedicate this book to my wife, Vicky Webster. For the past 30 years, she has given her entire life for the ministry as Head of School at Mount Airy Christian Academy. She is retiring this year and she well deserves a rest. She has tirelessly given of herself to this ministry, many times at great cost to herself. She has not asked for anything. At times she was not even paid due to the shortage of money. She cleaned the rest rooms several years to keep the school afloat. Hours were spent giving of herself for this cause. Only eternity knows the sacrifice and cost. That is the way she would want it.

Introduction

One of the most important sections of a book might well be the introduction. After all, it lets you know whether a book is worth your time, right? In our fast-paced culture, time is valuable. So let me give you some idea about how you'll spend your time with this book.

This journey began about 30 years ago, when by His grace I was blessed to develop a men's discipleship journey. During that study, I came across the marks of a disciple. I was deeply moved by the principles Jesus taught and how different my life seemed to be in comparison. These points are included in this study.

In addition, I have been blessed to travel all over the world and visit many different lands and meet many believers who live differently than we do in America. They do not see giving or serving as sacrifice; they see it as privilege. They *look* for opportunities that cost them, rather than running from cost. Some have even laid down their lives for the cause. One such visit in India brought this directly to my heart. I spent time with numerous pastors who had experienced direct attacks by the enemy for their faith. Their stories are forever etched into my mind. They had even written a song that told their stories. I remember crying as I heard them talk and sing. That aroused in me a deeper longing to live more of what Jesus taught.

Yet how is that possible in a society that neither requires much of a cost, nor preaches the need for one? This book is an attempt to tackle this dilemma that I faced. My prayer is that you would also embrace the teachings of the Savior and look at the idea of cost differently than ever before. May we all live more like Jesus taught.

"Jesus paid it all, all to Him I owe." So goes a line in a popular hymn written by Elvina Hall in 1865, just after the Civil War. It remains so popular that it is still a staple in contemporary Christian music today. Most of the time, people concentrate on the first part of the line. Jesus, after all, did pay it all. But how often do we pay attention to the last part of that lyric, ". . .all to

Him I owe"? What does that *all* mean, exactly? Are these words just something we sing? Are they even scriptural, or are they something a songwriter came up with to settle the intransigencies of meter and rhythm?

The truth is that we *do* owe Jesus all, and, as Scripture frequently tells us, we must be prepared to pay a cost—not for our salvation—but to live an effective life in Him. That cost demands our all. This book will attempt to evaluate that truth to the degree that Jesus meant for us to understand. May the Lord create in all of us a passion to live our lives in a way that honors Jesus in all we do.

Chapter 1

The Cost of Following Jesus from His Own Words

OUR SOCIETY IS ACCUSTOMED to paying for things. We constantly purchase items and charge them on our credit cards. Our desire for something often ignores the cost involved in having that item. We take that thing home and then later wonder why we purchased it. We call this "buyer's remorse." The reason buyer's remorse exists is that we often fail to count the cost.

This is not unlike many professing believers' spiritual journeys. They "buy in" to Jesus, accepting all the benefits of His salvation that come with His death on the cross, and thinking that it will just be a way to make their lives happier and more comfortable. Yet, as time goes on, they begin to realize the cost. Why would we even think that following Jesus throughout a lifetime would not involve a cost? This book will attempt to explain that there is indeed a cost to following Jesus. As a matter of fact, it will cost you your life.

We will examine the cost of following Jesus from three areas of the New Testament: the Gospels, the Book of Acts, and the Epistles. These three sections cover the first three eras of the church, including the teachings of Jesus, which form the foundation of the church (the Gospel accounts); the historical example of the early church (Acts); and the teachings (the Epistles) of the early followers concerning Jesus and the cost of following.

These three sections reveal several important truths. First, you will undeniably see that the cost of following Jesus is all throughout the New Testament. Second, you will see that the early church understood that exact teaching and actually lived the same. Third, you will see that after the start of the church, the writers of the New Testament also wrote exactly what Jesus had said earlier about the cost. In order to escape this teaching in the New Testament, one would have to either tear out much of the New Testament or simply rewrite it. Sadly, both are happening. Many large and small churches have either glossed over these passages or rewritten them. Some other churches have simply created a new Jesus altogether. Either we take the words for what they say, or we begin to make up a new Jesus that fits our current way of life.

If it is even possible to sum up Jesus' teachings, then these three truths just may do it for us:

1. All followers are called to live only for Christ.
2. All followers are called to sacrifice for Christ.
3. All followers are called to lose their lives for Christ. While they certainly "keep living," they now are living for a different call which implies "losing one's life."

These three statements are clear in the words of Jesus. They are clear in the book of Acts, in the example of Jesus, in the examples of the first followers, and in the writings of the apostles. Because they are so clear, the actions we need to take must be equally clear.

THE PROBLEM

Can we pause for just a moment here? Think over those three principles. Can you think of anyone you know who lives like that? Can you think of anyone you know who preaches like that? Does your life model those truths? In general, we are far busier loving the world than we are changing it. Therefore, we have reinvented a Jesus that makes it easier to be a Christian while we still claim to follow him. Let me illustrate it this way: if we can agree that Jesus taught the cost of following Him, then we should ask ourselves where that cost is today. We hear of believers living a life of comfort, ease, and pleasure, wanting a world that is driven by their wants and wishes rather than His commands. Either we have misinterpreted what Jesus said or we have reinvented Jesus. The Jesus of the New Testament does not look like the Jesus portrayed today by most in America. Perhaps because America today is more affluent than most of the world, we think we are entitled to a softer Jesus.

This problem is evident in the United States. Here are a few examples that we ought to examine. America, although a Christian nation in its roots, is hardly Christian in its behavior. We produce massive amounts of pornography. We have drug and alcohol problems. We are a leader in sex trafficking. We have kicked God out of the government-run schools, and abortion still continues to be a normal way of life. As of late, we have lost the definition of marriage (one man and one woman for life). We have reinvented sexuality and gender definitions.

Even professing believers are not immune to the shifts. The common language today of some believers resembles more of the proverbial sailors from ages past than it does someone who believes Christ is his Savior. Believers indulge in, and become addicted to, drugs, alcohol, and sex almost as much as nonbelievers. Bible reading, praying, witnessing, and other behaviors that should be the norm of followers of Jesus is more the behavior of the few. Additionally, daily time alone with God is becoming a lost art. Few even pray for more than a few minutes a day. True, none of these things *make* one a believer, but they are certainly elements that help the believer stand out from the rest of the world. The main question is this: How can we be salt and light in a world where one cannot distinguish the believer from the nonbeliever? Somehow, we have changed the cost of following Jesus for the desire to be in and of this present world.

Church has become a convenience. The idea of being faithful in church attendance and ministry is evaluated by whether there is something better to do. You cannot count on commitment if the world offers something "better." Giving sacrificially is rare. Giving today is more based on what individuals can afford to give after they have taken care of all their needs and wants. If they can spare a few dollars a month, that is their tithe. Many people have car payments far higher than their tithes. Serving can occur if it fits into a church member's schedule, but don't expect them to be in a small group or give up their time on other nights in the week. The behavior of Acts 2:41–47 seems foreign to the average church member today. It is more like a convenience-store faith than an Acts 2 committed faith.

This problem extends not only to individual believers but also to the way the church interacts in society. Do we need to wonder why the church has lost its influence in the world? We are so like the world that there is no room to influence. The church is fighting over sexuality. The church is fighting over music. The church is fighting over commitment. Instead of raising up an army of soldiers that is standing strong as a model of godly living, we are raising up a generation of individuals who hate having their comfort disturbed. No wonder the younger generation wants nothing to do with this view of Christ. It is soft and convictionless. As long as we keep selling a reinvented Jesus, we will continue to see a movement away from the true Jesus.

You, the reader, may be commended for *not* wanting a status quo faith. Maybe there are others out there who realize the tragic path we are on. Maybe this is not a lost cause. Maybe we can get back to the historical Jesus and the power of His Words. Maybe we once again can turn the world upside down.

THE CALL

There is no better place to begin this study than with a general overview of Jesus' teachings concerning the cost of following Him. If Jesus is our Example, Role Model, Leader, and so much more, then we cannot live for Him without a clear understanding of who He is and what He taught. Keep in mind that although these verses were first directed to His disciples in His day, they certainly apply to all of us as well.

In order to fully appreciate the New Testament writings after Jesus, it is imperative that we examine Jesus' last command. This last command is found in Matthew 28:18–20. Let me put in here in its entirety:

> And Jesus came and spoke to them, saying, All authority has been given to me in heaven and on earth. Go therefore, and make disciples of all the nations, baptizing them in the name of the Father, and of the Son, and of the Holy Spirit: Teaching them to observe all things that I have commanded you:and, lo, I am with you always, even to the end of the age. Amen.

Notice several very important principles from this passage. The disciples were to go into all the world. They were to teach (the actual verb here is *to make disciples*) and baptize all nations. They were even told what they were to teach: the commands of Jesus. The verb *teaching* in verse 20 is an aorist Greek verb. This aorist tense verb implies that Jesus is referring to the teachings that He has *already* given to them, not some new teaching that they were to discover. So Jesus taught them to go into all the world and make disciples, teaching everyone everywhere all that He had previously taught them. That would give the first missionary disciples the exact curriculum that they would need. To further ensure that His teachings would be preserved just as He had spoken them, He inspired writers to write exactly what He taught (2 Tim. 3:16, 2 Pet. 1:21). Additionally, He gave them the Holy Spirit who would bring to remembrance all things that they had been taught by Jesus. Listen to the words of John 14:26: "But the Helper, the Holy Spirit, whom the Father will send in My name, He will teach you all things, and bring to your remembrance all things that I said to you." He wanted to be sure that all His commands were taught and preserved. The apostles taught these commands and recorded them for us in books called the Epistles. Therefore, in order to understand the Epistles, we need a firm grasp of the Gospel accounts. That truth compels us to understand Jesus' teachings with greater commitment than ever.

AN OVERVIEW OF JESUS' TEACHING ON THE COST OF FOLLOWING HIM

Please note that some of these statements are forceful, while others are implied. Also, a few of these are listed multiple times since the Gospel writers repeated the theme in their accounts. Nevertheless, the sheer volume speaks much to the subject. The expanded list, with Scripture references, is found in Appendix 1. Here are some summary details of that list.

1. He called men to follow Him, which implied leaving what they owned and what they were doing. They understood the cost and did exactly that—left it all.
2. His call implied not going back to their past. When they try it in John 21, He is there to remind them of the call.
3. He challenged them about the dangers of the treasures of this earth. He realized the potential that the world had to pull at their hearts.
4. There were no middle choices in the call. Either they followed Him, or they followed self. No man is capable of having more than one Master. Even His use of *Master* implies ownership and rulership.
5. As He calls us to seek Him first, it is clear that it is not "first" as in "first on a list." But it is "first and foremost." No other gods.
6. His teaching on the narrow way reminded them of the cost.
7. Some came to Him and wanted to follow, but they also had their own agenda. He had nothing to do with that kind of following.
8. One obvious example of the cost was when Matthew left his lucrative career of tax collecting. He left that lifestyle for one of wandering homelessness.
9. We will look at the multiple passages that talk of taking one's own cross, dying to self, and forsaking all later in the study. These certainly teach the cost.

10. John the Baptist, the forerunner of Jesus, is martyred. No question his death resonated regularly in the minds of Jesus' followers. This journey will cost.

11. The disciples would have listened regularly as Jesus engaged those who wanted to follow. One example that surely captured their minds had to be when He told the rich man to sell all and give it away.

12. The disciples later reminded Jesus that they had left all, which shows that they truly did.

13. Some of the terms Jesus used for them had to have hit home the idea of cost. *Servant* is the most pronounced; it could be translated as *slave*.

14. Why would He promise His forever presence with us if this journey was going to be easy?

15. In one of His teachings, He even mentioned the cost of severing a hand or removing an eye. Now, we know this was not to be taken literally, but what a message it must have sent.

16. On one occasion, He told a man who wanted to follow and who had kept the Law that he still lacked total surrender to Jesus.

17. When the widow gives her all, He commends her. Was that an example to them of the cost?

18. He often taught that persecution is coming.

19. He informed his disciples that they would not be received.

20. As He washed their feet, what overall things do you suspect He was trying to get them to discover?

21. He taught that He was sending them out as lambs before wolves, implying a cost.

22. He talked of how following Him would bring about family division. Family was huge to this culture.

23. He taught many "extreme" statements such as being last, giving all, selling all, serving all, dying to all, abandoning life, etc. Did He ever teach that it would be comfortable to follow him?

24. He led them by example on the subject of humility. Their pride had to go.

25. His whole teaching on losing their lives certainly informed them that this following of Jesus would cost them.

26. In one example after hard teaching, some of His disciples left Him. He let them go.
27. He even used the strong word *hate* to set the standard high for cost.
28. He also used the highest of all words for love to remind them that this following would put their deepest emotions to the test.
29. He included the idea of laying down one's life in His teaching. Would that not imply cost?
30. He made it clear to them that they were not to be of this world. Yet the world calls us daily. He was setting up the cost principles for them.

This is quite a list! The complete list found in the appendix is rather overwhelming, to say the least. We will look at His cost and the disciples' costs later, but it is not a stretch to say that Jesus relentlessly taught the cost of following Him. Yet we think of a Jesus without cost, one who just wants us to be happy, to make life more comfortable. Which one is this the real biblical call?

Just how much evidence to support a premise is considered enough? Truthfully, if Jesus said something one time, that should be sufficient for us. But for our Lord to teach this theme in the combined Gospels some 73 times is staggering. Even if some on the list could be removed because of ambiguity, there are still substantial references to support the idea. The Lord stressed in many different ways that following Him will cost you. It will cost you your life (lose your life). It will cost you your wants and desires (hate your life). It will cost you your treasures (lay up in Heaven). It will cost you your all (forsake all). What is really left?

That cost, as we will see, is worth all and more. Jesus did not call on us to pay that cost because He had some desire to watch us flagellate ourselves and wallow in earthly misery. The cost of following Him leads to an amazingly blessed life, a life that is truly worth living. We need to remember what a privilege it is to serve the Lord. Can you think of anything that you do that is even close to the high calling of serving the Lord? Can you imagine bowing before Him one day and Him receiving the honor for the life we have lived fully for Him? That is what we call "no regret" Christianity.

TAKING THE CHAPTER A BIT FURTHER

1. Pick Matthew or Luke and read through it in one sitting, focusing particularly on the last hours of Jesus' life, and reflect on the enormous price He paid.

2. Do you see any other passages from the Gospel account that you read that could be added to Appendix 1?
3. Read Acts 2:41–47. List as many priorities of the early believers as you can find. How many of these are priorities of God's people today?
4. Take one of the stronger passages and do a more in-depth study of it—perhaps either Matthew 10:1–38, 16:24–26, 20:26–28, Luke 9:23–6, or 14:25–33. By "in depth study," I mean looking up definitions of some of the words, reading the parallel passages, asking questions about the passage, and specifically asking God what He wants you to learn from them. For example, when He says, "Deny yourself," ask "How do we do that in a world that is so self-focused?" Or when Jesus says "hate," ask "Why would Jesus tell me to hate?"

Chapter 2

Jesus Lived the Cost

If you've been exposed to any sort of Christian teaching, you probably know that Jesus provided the model for the ways in which we should live, relate to God, and relate to one another. Does it surprise you to know that He also modeled living a life of cost as well? In fact, the costs He had to pay, even beyond our usual focal point of the cross, are beyond anything any of us have had to bear! This chapter emphasizes the life Jesus lived on this earth. He left the splendor of Heaven and laid aside glory (John 17:5). Can any of us fully understand what exactly that all entailed? Since that may be far beyond our scope, let's just examine the Gospels for the specifics of the cost that He lived while on the earth.

HIS BIRTH

Keep in mind that Jesus is God. God will again take residence on this earth. Everyone should know about this! True, a star shone over Bethlehem as a sign of the Messiah's arrival, but it came after His birth, and the only ones who noticed it were some distant rulers who were not even Jewish! Jesus received both visitors and very costly gifts, but they also arrived after His birth. Jesus' parents were peasants, and we know this by the inexpensive choice of offering for the birth in Luke 2:23–24. He was born in a stable, a cave, or an area similar in nature. We gather this from the fact that his parents laid Him in a manger—a feeding trough for animals. His only immediate visitors were shepherds, and people did not regard shepherds as respected citizens. Jesus was born without the privilege of even a room in the local inn, and not long after His birth, He and His parents had to flee from their home because His life was placed in danger. His incredibly unassuming birth, humble even by the standards of that time, already shows that Jesus paid a cost. He should have been given the fanfare befitting the King of Kings.

HIS EARLY YEARS

Jesus grew up in a typical Jewish home as best as we can ascertain. One truth recorded about those years is that He put Himself under the subjection of His parents (Luke 2:51). Now, keep in mind we are talking about God Almighty, clothed in human flesh, who submitted to sinful mankind.

In addition, the Bible reveals that Jesus' brothers did not believe in Him. We can only imagine what transpired in that home. Most likely, you have either seen or participated in sibling rivalry. Each family has its own share of diverse personalities and conflicts. Some parents may *think* that their offspring is the "perfect child" who could never do anything wrong, but Jesus actually *was* perfect; He was the sinless one! Can you imagine how much that irritated His siblings? The gospels record that they were impatient with Him and even considered Him crazy at one point (Mark 3:21). Clearly, they did not take Him seriously even as an adult, and He had to live with that on a daily basis.

One element of cost is more implied than stated, and it involves Jesus' earthly father, Joseph. The gospels do not mention Joseph at all after the first years of Jesus' life. We do know that while Jesus hung on the cross, He committed His mother, Mary, to His disciple John (John 19:26–27). Undoubtedly, Jesus ensured she was taken care of, which He would not have needed to do if Joseph was still around. It's possible, therefore, that Jesus grew up in a single-parent household. Could there be some cost in that? Just consider any child who has had to grow up in that kind of circumstance. If Joseph did die sometime during Jesus' younger years, then as the oldest son, Jesus would have had to take over some of the responsibility of the family. Leaving the family to go into ministry surely would not have gone over well. All of this could have brought some level of cost to Him personally.

HIS MINISTRY YEARS

He Was Often Alone

Jesus' ministry years on this earth were, by our standards, quite brief. Although they encompassed a small portion of His life on Earth, these years were incredibly significant. During that short time, the Lord paid a huge price in many areas that we consider essential. Socially, emotionally, and physically, Jesus suffered in ways that may surprise people who are accustomed to seeing illustrations of Him holding little children, healing people, and blessing bread with a halo of light around His head.

For instance, think of the loneliness He had to endure. During His ministry, Jesus was often alone. Sometimes, this was because He deliberately withdrew in order to have better communion with His Father (Matt 14:1–13, 23, Mark 1:35–36, 6:30–32, 46, Luke 5:16, 6:12, 9:18, John 6:15, 7:10). Even then, choosing solitude was costly. It was very difficult for Him to get away—He often exhausted Himself trying to do so! But other times, even when He needed support, He didn't have it. Matthew 26:36–56 talks about how Jesus took His disciples to the Garden of Gethsemane to pray before His crucifixion. He specifically asked them to pray, but they slept instead (v. 43). In fact, this happened several times for hours! When Jesus really needed them to strengthen themselves and draw closer to Him, they let Him pray alone. And think about this: He often was alone even in crowds of people who simply didn't understand Him (see the next section). Many of us know that feeling of intense loneliness that can come when we're in the middle of a crowd of people with whom we have no real connection. Imagine how much of a stranger Jesus felt in a world that rejected Him. He paid a tremendous cost in leaving the perfect Heaven to take on the limitations of an earthly existence where He was truly alone.

He Was Often Misunderstood

Besides being alone, Jesus was often misunderstood when He was with others. Remember that Jesus is truth and speaks truth (John 14:6). He cannot do anything but that which is true. However, He often was misunderstood and judged for it. Let's check out the Gospel of Matthew to illustrate this. Some of the people in this list just didn't understand. Others deliberately misunderstood Him out of a desire to resist His teachings. Overall, many seem to have not known who He was, even after everything He showed them and did for them.

1. Misunderstood by Satan (Matt 4:1–11): For Satan to even challenge Jesus was sheer madness. A created being successfully confronting the Creator—not going to happen. Satan took his best shots and got nowhere, including his attacks of "if thou be." Satan knew who He was. But he just did not understand how all of this would end.

2. Misunderstood by "His own city" (Matt 9:1–3): His own city concluded "this man blasphemes," greatly misunderstanding Jesus' message.
3. Misunderstood by the Pharisees (Matt 9:11): This is the first example of it in Matthew, but a careful reading of the Gospels will reveal numerous times that the Pharisees (sometimes alone and sometimes with other leaders) would either accuse Jesus or attempt to trick Him in some way (12:2, 14, 24, 15:2, 16:1, 19:3, 22:15, 34, 23:13).
4. Misunderstood by John's disciples (Matt 9:14): Here, they question Jesus about fasting as if they are trying to distinguish between Jesus' disciples and John's. Clearly, they did not know better.
5. Misunderstood by a ruler's friends and family (Matt 9:24): Jesus came to the ruler's house to do a miracle. A certain ruler's daughter had died, and he had requested that Jesus raise his daughter back to life. He seemed to have more faith in Jesus than even the disciples did. When Jesus arrived, He said that the girl was not dead but asleep. The verse further records, "They laughed Him to scorn." So, Jesus proceeded to send the people out of the room and then healed the girl. Who had the last laugh?
6. Misunderstood by John the Baptist (Matt 11:1–3): Even though John had pointed out Jesus earlier at the baptism and called Him the Lamb of God who takes away the sin of the world (John 1:29), he later asked who Jesus is. Maybe John just wanted to be sure in a period of discouragement, but John misunderstood.
7. Misunderstood by the generation (Matt 11:16–19): Jesus talked about this generation in verse 16, saying they had accused Him of being "gluttonous, and a winebibber, a friend of tax collectors, and sinners." Of course, the latter half is accurate, but He was certainly not gluttonous or a winebibber. They seemed to not care if these things were true or not. They truly misunderstood.
8. Misunderstood by Chorazin, Bethsaida, and Capernaum (Matt 11:20–24): Mighty works were done in these cities, but the people did not respond to the truth. Did they not know? Or did they just misunderstand?
9. Misunderstood by the Synagogue attendees (Matt 12:10): Jesus went into the synagogue as was often His agenda, and they questioned Him so that they might accuse Him. Did they actually think they were going to get an edge on Him this way? They completely misunderstood the Person they were engaging.

10. Misunderstood by the people (Matt 12:23): In verse 22, the blind and dumb both spoke and saw. In response, the people were amazed. Yet was just Jesus at work.

11. Misunderstood by His family (Matt 12:46–50): Jesus had now been away from His family and in full ministry for a while, and so His family came to see Him. Nothing states why they came—just that they desired to speak with Him (v. 46). It would seem as if He did not even stop what He was doing to engage them. He faced a deep cost with His family.

12. Misunderstood by His disciples (Matt 13:10): Here, the text seems to imply that the disciples questioned why He taught in parables as if they did not approve. If that is the case, they greatly misunderstood Him and why He came.

13. Misunderstood by His own country (Matt 13:54–58): Verse 54 says He came into His own country, and in the following verse, they also questioned who He was. They were offended by Him, and because of their unbelief, He did not perform many mighty works there.

14. Misunderstood by Herod (Matt 14:2): When Herod heard of the fame of Jesus, he concluded that He was John the Baptist, risen from the dead. John had clearly specified that he was not Jesus, but Herod obviously misunderstood.

15. Misunderstood by the multitudes (Matt 15:31): Great multitudes came to Jesus while He was on a nearby mountain. They brought many sick people to Him, and He healed them. Although the end of verse 31 says that they glorified God, the earlier part of the verse claims that they also "wondered."

16. Misunderstood by Peter (Matt 16:22): Jesus explained to the disciples that He would travel to Jerusalem to suffer and die. Peter took Jesus aside and rebuked Him, evidently still misunderstanding who He was and why He came.

17. Misunderstood by those who collected tribute (Matt 17:24): The tribute collectors did not even approach Jesus. They instead asked Peter whether Jesus paid tribute. Jesus silenced them as He did with all who tried to challenge Him.

18. Misunderstood by the rich young ruler (Matt 19:22): The unnamed ruler came to Jesus, and he tried to persuade the Lord that he was certainly a good man and worthy of eternity in Heaven. Jesus told him to give away all his treasure to the poor and follow Him. The ruler chose

his riches over Jesus. Truly, he would later regret this decision because he misunderstood.

19. Misunderstood by James, John, and their mother (Matt 20:20): John, James, and their mother brought an interesting request to Jesus. The brothers desired to sit with Him in His kingdom, one at His right hand and the other at His left. Of course, Jesus rebuked them for it and turned the situation into a lesson on servanthood. The brothers and their mother misunderstood the One whom they were following.
20. Misunderstood by the chief priests and scribes (Matt 21:15): What an unusual verse this is! Let me share it with you in its entirety: "And when the chief priests and scribes saw the wonderful things that he did, and the children crying in the temple, and saying, 'Hosanna to the son of David'; they were sore displeased" (Matt 21:15, KJV). Now, what am I missing here? They saw the wonderful things that He did and yet were displeased. Their response is undoubtedly a result of misunderstanding.
21. Misunderstood by the Sadducees (Matt 22:23): This group of religious leaders did not believe in a resurrection at all. So, they asked Jesus about the resurrection. Were they simply ignorant, or did they just misunderstand?
22. Misunderstood by Jerusalem (Matt 23:37): In this verse, Jesus offers a rebuke to Jerusalem, which decidedly refers, not to the city, but to its inhabitants. He states that He would have gathered them together unto Himself had they not resisted. These people also misunderstood Him.

Here, I have listed 22 different occasions in Matthew alone where Jesus was misunderstood by those with whom He was in direct contact. Maybe some of the misunderstandings were deliberate, and maybe some people were simply confused. Either way, Jesus came to enlighten the world and bring truth, and to have so many misunderstand Him undoubtedly must have been part of His cost. Can we even imagine how hard it was for Him to be Truth and yet be so misunderstood?

He Was Limited

This is a difficult area to address because there are so many different views of the hypostatic union (the combination of Jesus' divine and human natures in one Person) and all that is involved. Several things, however, are evident. First, He was always God. Second, He did not stop being God at any time while here on the earth. Third, He never lost any of that which makes

Him God. However, He limited Himself in some capacity that is beyond my understanding. Although omnipresent, He was in a body. Although omniscient, He made statements suggesting limitations. Although omnipotent, He experienced hunger, thirst, and sleep. Because this area is so difficult, maybe it is best to just state my thoughts and leave it up to each reader to discern. Just keep in mind that whatever you conclude, if it takes away from Him being fully God, then the conclusion is inaccurate. Regardless, there is some kind of cost in this limitation.

He Lacked Earthly Comforts

It is probably best to not overstate this section, but remember that He is God and only knew of the splendor of Heaven. He left all of that to be "confined" to a body with all the earthly trials that entails. He even took it further by restricting Himself on many levels. He had no place to lay His head. He never owned property. He was always borrowing, whether it was a boat, a house, a donkey, a room for Passover, or a tomb. He had a limited wardrobe, and even His final attire was gambled for at the cross. He left earth without ever owning a thing. It was His lifestyle, but it was a lifestyle with a tremendous cost.

Jesus came to impact this world, and He succeeded. But "He came unto His own, and His own received Him not" (John 1:11). How troublesome that must have been for Him. His life was regularly full of cost. It shouldn't surprise us that our lives will be costly, as well.

TAKING THE CHAPTER A BIT FURTHER

1. Discover the meaning of the hypostatic union. How does it apply to your life personally?
2. Pick a passage from the Gospels where Jesus' humanity and deity seem to be in conflict. Then, explain how this apparent conflict can be resolved.
3. What do you make of the truth that Jesus lived on this earth without many of the luxuries of this life? Does it teach us anything by example, or was it something that was just normal for that time?

Chapter 3

Jesus' Death Proves There Was a Cost

After reading about His life, if you cannot see that He paid a truly great cost for us, then perhaps you will be convinced upon examining His last hours. The betrayal, arrests, trials, abuse, and crucifixion Jesus had to endure historically encompass the most horrible hours anyone has ever experienced in that short amount of time—from 6:00 p.m. on a Thursday until 6:00 p.m. the following day. This roughly 24 hours will reveal the cost and horror of that experience. It explains why Isaiah questioned whether Jesus was even a human after they had finished with Him (Isa. 52:14) and why Jesus told Mary, "Behold your son" (John 19:26). Despite knowing Him better than anyone, she would have looked at that disfigured body and wondered herself. Just imagine the beatings, the beard plucked out, the thorns, and the scourging. He didn't just die for us—He paid a huge cost in the process.

THE COST OF THE BETRAYAL

The first area to examine is the betrayal of Jesus. Have you ever been betrayed by someone? Many of us have felt betrayal at one time or another, and it hurts. But was it a person whom you had personally invested time in or someone whom you had greatly helped and poured your life into? Have you ever been betrayed by someone who sold you out for money and then led the enemy right to you? Have you ever been betrayed by someone who plotted your capture? Or maybe someone who assisted in your arrest and ultimately your death? If these are not true of you, you may not fully understand the cost of being betrayed in this manner in the way Jesus experienced it.

This betrayal began with the agreement to hand Jesus over to the soldiers for the price of a common slave (30 pieces of silver). We know that Judas loved money (John 12:6). He was a thief who kept the money bag for the disciples. Talk about the fox guarding the chicken coop!

Eventually, a plan was fleshed out. Judas would lead a band of soldiers to arrest Jesus in the Garden of Gethsemane. Here, Jesus spent His final hours before His arrest, His eleven disciples accompanying Him while He prayed in the garden. The prayer was so intense that at one time, He forced blood through His pores (Luke 22:44). His disciples all fell asleep during His first two prayer sessions, including His inner circle of Peter, James, and John. They didn't realize that a net was being cast around them. But Jesus knew. He was fully aware. After His final time of prayer, Judas entered the Garden with the soldiers.

The following scene is rather intense. Jesus revealed who He is by calling Himself the "I AM," and they all immediately fell down (John 18:6). Peter then tried to fend off the estimated 600 soldiers but only succeeded in cutting off the ear of one named Malchus, whom Jesus immediately healed. (Before we ridicule Peter for this, we need to remember that the disciples possessed two swords, and Peter was the only one willing to at least attempt a defense. We can only speculate who held the other sword. However, the text does not state whether the other armed disciple attempted any resistance.)

Afterwards, Jesus was taken by the soldiers to the trials, which lasted from Thursday night to Friday morning. What did Judas do from this point forward? Well we know he visited the religious leaders and tried to show some remorse, but they laughed at him, so he hanged himself. This is a tragic end for a man whom Jesus had said would have been better off if he had never been born. (Matt 26:24)

But even in the midst of this craziness, we need to keep in mind that all of this came at a great price to the Savior. He handpicked Judas after an all-night prayer meeting and then trained him for three years. He involved Judas in every major event in His life, including the teachings and miracles. If you have ever invested your life into someone, and they turned against you in some fashion, then you may have some idea of the cost of leadership and investing. Not all attempts turn out well. Of course, we know this was part of Jesus' plan, but from a human perspective, this betrayal was a great cost.

THE COST OF HIS TRIALS

After Jesus was arrested in the Garden of Gethsemane, He was taken through a series of trials that would have lasted through the night and into the next morning. These trials were a mockery of everything that should have been done to secure a proper verdict. Three of these trials were religious, while the other three were civil. However, all of them were illegal. Robert Robinson explains quite a number of the infractions of Jewish Law of that day; the following are summarized from his "Six Illegal Trials":

> Jesus was interrogated without being charged with anything. Annas, who directed the first trial, was the former High Priest, but he had no right to question from a legal perspective. It was against the Law to question someone at night, to hit a prisoner who was being interrogated, and to bear false witnesses. No trial could be held in any place other than the Council Chamber in the Temple. They were not to accuse the one on trial, and they were supposed to be fair.
>
> Furthermore, no trials should have been held on feast days, and yet Jesus' trial fell on the Passover. The Sanhedrin never polled for a verdict. Someone should have represented the accuser. Twenty-four hours were supposed to have passed between the verdict and a sentence, and if found guilty, then the prisoner was to have another three days before the execution. Fasting also should have occurred before the sentence. During the trials, they changed the charge from blasphemy to treason, which was not permitted by Law. Pilate kept Jesus under arrest, even though he found nothing wrong with Him. Herod never accused Him of anything, which meant He should have been released. Pilate allowed an innocent man to be crucified.[1]

All of the above were express violations of Jewish Law and strictly forbidden. Much of our criminal law today comes from Jewish Law, and it has greatly benefitted the accused. The idea of innocent until proven guilty remains reasonable. However, this was no fair trial on any level. Those who arrested Him had an agenda that Jesus would never be released. Because they had Him now, He was going to die. So, let's do a quick review of the six trials.

1. Robinson, Robert Clifton. "Six Illegal Trials."

Trial #1

His first trial was before Annas (Matt 26:67–68, Mark 14:65, Luke 22:63–64, John 18:12–14). Annas was not the present high priest, but he had much power through his son-in-law, Caiaphas, who was the high priest. During this first trial, at least nine different things happened to Jesus. They spat in His face (Matt 26:67). Notice that the subject is plural, suggesting it was not just one, but several. How degrading this must have been—how humiliating. This is God whom they spat on. The text then says they buffeted Him (Matt 26:67). Again, notice the plural. This is the same word used in 2 Corinthians 12:7 to describe what Satan does to us with a thorn in the flesh. So, they gave Jesus a Satanic hit and intentionally struck with their fists. He was pulverized. Afterwards, they struck Him with the palms of their hands (Matt 26:67). The noun is still plural. Undoubtedly, it was not a gentle slap. They mocked Him and asked Him to prophesy (Matt 26:68), making fun of Him and laughing in His face.

Mark further records the circumstances of this trial. They blindfolded Him (Mark 14:65), and we can speculate their reasoning behind this. Was it because the beatings became so horrific that it was easier to hit Him without seeing His face? They didn't know that a blindfold can't deter God. Luke's account says that they held Him (Luke 22:63), and *held* is an intensive verb. Paul also used it in 2 Corinthians 5:14 to say the love of Christ constrained him. Probably several people held Him, a tactical way to keep Him upright and hit Him harder. It bears the same mentality as the idea "You hold Him so I can hit Him." Luke adds that they mocked Him again (Luke 22:63) and then beat Him (Luke 22:63). The text seems to imply a different beating than before. The verb is a present active participle, which implies ongoing beatings—hit after hit after hit. This is the same word used in Acts 5:40 to describe the beating of the apostles. Neither would have been a gentle beating. Finally, Luke states that they blasphemously spoke against Him (Luke 22:65). It is hard to know what all of that fully entails, but we can be confident it was severe.

The torment was only just beginning in that first trial. Also, it seems like the most logical place to assume that Jesus turned and looked upon Peter here. The possibility is not absolute, but it does fit well. Only Luke records this for us in Luke 22:54–62. Peter had followed Jesus into the areas of the trials and was warming himself by the fire. After the third denial when the rooster crowed, Jesus looked upon Peter. Remember that this was after His beatings. No wonder Peter ran out and wept bitterly. Can you imagine the cost of having your prized pupil curse and swear that he never even knew you?

Trial #2

Jesus was then carried to Caiaphas (John 18:24). Annas sent Jesus to him bound. Where did they think He would go? This was just one more attempt to humiliate Jesus. The text does not offer much about this trial. It was simply short as Caiaphas must have been too busy with his official priestly responsibility with Passover, yet here he had *the* Passover Lamb right in his midst. There may have been more abuse here, but the text just does not say.

Trial #3

After Caiaphas, Jesus appeared before the Sanhedrin (Luke 22:66–71). Seemingly, not all of them were present, especially if you consider that some were believers in Jesus, such as Joseph of Arimathea. Here, He again faced more acts against Him, although this round was mild and in front of the official court. Keep in mind that the Jews could not put Him to death, but they could choose to inflict pain. Also, they knew this was their last shot, so although the text may not record much detail, it leaves room for interpretation.

Trial #4:

Jesus was then sent off for the civil components of the trials. His first stop took place before Pilate (Matt 27:1–2, 11, Mark 15:1–5, Luke 23:1–5, and John 18:28–38). The Jews could not kill Jesus, so they needed an official sentence. Pilate had no love for the Jews, especially not for someone claiming to be the King of the Jews. They bound Him as He was led to Pilate (Matt 27:2) and then interrogated (Mark 15:3–5). We do not know what they did to Him here, but we do know they falsely accused Jesus (Luke 23:2). Pilate found no fault in Him. When he heard that Jesus came from Galilee, he hastily sent Him over to Herod, who happened to be in Jerusalem at that time.

Trial #5

Only Luke records this event for us (Luke 23:8–12). Herod was glad to see Jesus and hoped He would perform a sign, and so the soldiers poked at and mocked Him. He was questioned at length (Luke 23:9). They vehemently accused Him (Luke 23:10). Actually, it is better to say that they were vehemently accusing Him as an ongoing event. Can you just imagine them yelling in His face? The text says that they treated Him with contempt (Luke 23:11), and the KJV specifies, "they set Him at naught," which means to despise Him, to regard Him as nothing (Luke 18:9). Remember that these were trained soldiers. They were trained killers. They were trained torturers. Their treatment of Jesus could not have been pleasant.

Trial #6

Finally, the trials came to an end (Matt 27:15–31a, Mark 15:3–20a, Luke 23:16–25, John 18:39–19:16a). These passages store plenty of information. This last trial was the most detailed of them all, written about by each of the four gospel writers, who described it as rather horrific.

Matthew 27:17 says they set Him on the same level as the criminal named Barabbas. Then, they stripped Jesus and dressed Him in a scarlet robe (Matt 27:28) and a crown of thorns (Matt 27:29). Is there any way to even imagine how painful that must have been? Afterwards, they placed a reed in His hand, bowed before Him (Matt 27:29), and then spat on Him (Matt 27:30). Have you ever been spat on? The verb here implies that this happened more than one time. Probably several of the soldiers engaged in this manner. Once they had mocked and spat on Jesus, they took the reed and struck Him on the head continuously (Matt 27:30). This is the same word used to describe Paul's beating in Acts 21:32. In that passage they almost beat him to death.

Matthew then adds that they mocked Him again and stripped Him (Matt 27:31). This was several times now He had been mocked and made fun of. Finally, Mark 15:15 states that they scourged Him. The text does not detail the scourging, but with the level of hatred that was around these trials, it was undoubtedly a horrible scene. If you saw the movie *The Passion of the Christ*, you may have seen a glimpse of what the scourging could have been like. The director of this movie explained that the whipping had to be toned down because people could not endure watching it. Imagine how terrible this suffering must have been.

A scourge in this day was a whip with pieces of bone or pottery embedded in the end. The whip would catch on the flesh and tear with every lash. The impact of multiple hits would surely leave the body in mere strips of flesh and exposed innards. Isaiah 50:6 gives some graphic details as well. Jesus' back and cheeks were given to the smiters. They plucked out His beard and spat on His face. Isaiah further adds in 52:14 that no one could recognize Him as a man. This was all part of His cost for coming to earth and making Himself vulnerable to sinful man.

By this point, it was early morning on Friday. The trials were over, and Jesus had stayed up all night, beaten, whipped, and torn apart. His body must have already entered some form of shock. Just think about how this horrific action was carried out by the very people He came to save. Can any of us truly understand what great cost He experienced even prior to the actual crucifixion? All of this He did because of His great love for us. Hallelujah, what a Savior.

THE COST OF THE CRUCIFIXION

Jesus had now been sentenced and prepared for His final journey on this earth, the walk to Calvary. This road has often been called the *Via Delarosa*, which is Latin for the way of grief, sorrow, or suffering. If you visit Israel today, you can walk the very path that many believe to be the same one Jesus took. It is a winding route from the Antonia Fortress to where Calvary is believed to be, with an approximate distance of 2000 feet. Keep in mind that Jesus was compelled to walk this after having no sleep, enduring the trials and the whipping, and receiving no food or water. All of it was meant to humiliate Him. While this story is found in all four Gospels, we will focus primarily on Luke's writing.

Luke 23:25 starts our discussion with a rather conclusive statement: "But he delivered Jesus to their will." This truly sets the stage for the rest of this sad story. Though the verse says Jesus was delivered to their will, we must remember that this statement is in fact not true. This was His will all along, and the more accurate view is He delivered Himself to them.

Before we dig into what we know to be true, let us reflect on some questions we may have after reading the text. How long did He carry the cross? Why did they compel someone else to carry it? How much of the cross did He actually carry? Who was Simon of Cyrene? Where were the disciples? These and many others are questions that may puzzle a reader focused on the details. Do not let the unknown clutter your mind so that you miss the facts. The description of the crucifixion is painful enough for us to see the cost He paid on our behalf.

Here is what appears to have happened. Jesus was physically exhausted and beaten down. He was still human. He still hungered and thirsted. He still felt the pain of every step He took. He likely reached the gate at the entrance to Jerusalem. The time was around 9:00 a.m., and the people would have been entering the city to celebrate Passover. How ironic it is that the Passover Lamb left Jerusalem as the people arrived to kill their Passover lambs for their own sin.

As He carried the cross, He probably moved too slowly for the Roman soldiers. They became impatient. Therefore, they forced someone to carry it for Him. He would have carried His cross all the way, but they wanted Him to move faster. So, they grabbed a man named Simon of Cyrene from the crowd. Was this a random pick? Doubtful. Cyrene was in Northern Africa, which could be present-day Libya. It is possible that the man who carried the cross was a non-Jew and also a different color, perhaps even black. Would it not be just like the Savior to do just that? He loved to break down all kinds of barriers—whether they dealt with gender or race—regardless of the cost.

The text offers more information about this mysterious man. The trip from Cyrene to Jerusalem may have been 800 miles. We learn from Mark 15:21 that Simon was the father of Alexander and Rufus. The name Alexander is mentioned six times in the New Testament, so we are not sure who they all were. Rufus is also mentioned here and in Romans 16:13. Are these all the same people? The only reason why it might be relevant here is that it would seem that these two men were believers. If so, and if Simon was recognized as their father, he might not have been a believer. Again, that would seem very fitting for one to carry the cross who was not a believer, not a Jew, and not white. Only God could work in such a way.

A great multitude followed Him, including women and children (Luke 23:27). Who exactly was in this crowd is not evident. More than likely, it contained some who were mentioned later at the cross, such as His mother and John. The women who mourned and lamented could very well have been paid mourners who often attended such occasions. Interestingly, they were not the only ones mourning. Luke 19:41 says that just a few days earlier, Jesus entered Jerusalem—maybe at the very same spot—and wept.

Then, Jesus turned to the mourners and told them not to weep for Him but for themselves and their children (Luke 22:28). What did He know was coming for them? Was this a hint to the destruction of Jerusalem just 40 or so years in the future? Or maybe it is much later when the Tribulation will be upon them, and they will ask for the mountains to fall on them (Luke 22:30). Regardless, He clearly says that they need to mourn because of what awaits them.

Luke also adds that there were two criminals who traveled with Jesus to the crucifixion (Luke 22:32). This fulfilled the prophecy in Isaiah 53:12, which reads He "was numbered with the transgressors." If crucifying the Son of God was not enough, they chose to do so right between two criminals, and Jesus even took the place of another criminal named Barabbas. Can you begin to see the depth of the price our Savior paid? He paid the ultimate cost.

It is rather interesting that little is explained about the crucifixion of Jesus in the Gospel narratives. The text states it rather simply in Luke 23:33: "And when they had come to the place called Calvary, there they crucified Him, and the criminals, one on the right hand and the other on the left." This offers very few details about crucifixion and what that entailed for our Savior. The text will later give us information of Jesus on the cross, but we have to gain the specifics elsewhere, such as exact descriptions about the nails and pieces of the cross. The crucifixion was just too somber of an event for Scripture to add any details. He was crucified. Let that sink in. It should have been our cross, but He was willing to pay the cost for us.

Once Jesus was on the cross, He made at least seven different statements. We only know of these seven because that is all the New Testament records for us, although there may have been more. The following lists His statements in order:

Statement 1: "Father, forgive them, for they know not what they do."
Luke 23:34

What was this statement all about? Well, we know what it does not mean. It was not about universal salvation or some clemency to all of mankind. It was also not some forgiveness of those who nailed Jesus to the cross. This was so much more. It appears to be a statement of forgiveness that is now available because of what He was about to do. This forgiveness, which is now open for all to accept and experience, was offered to the Father on behalf of everyone who would believe. Have you received forgiveness for your sins and have salvation in Jesus? The "them" in this verse is for all who believe.

After His first statement, the soldiers gambled for the only possession He had on this earth—His clothes. Typical clothing in that day would have included five different pieces: sandals, a robe-like garment, a headpiece, a belt, and a tunic. Jesus' tunic was gambled for, leaving us no idea of what may have happened to His other pieces of clothing. He came into the world with nothing and left the same—a good reminder for all of us. Hold on to the world's goods lightly as they are all fleeting and simply a vapor.

Statement #2: "Today, you will be with Me in Paradise."
Luke 23:43

This statement was made to one of the thieves on the cross next to Him. Clearly, Jesus was telling the man that something good was waiting, particularly being with Him.

Statement #3: "Woman, behold thy Son." John 19:26

There has been much discussion on what exactly this meant. Was it a direct command for John to take His mother with him from that day forward (which he did)? Was it a statement to Mary to consider John her son? Or was it His effort to make sure His mother knew it was Jesus Himself on the cross?

The last suggestion makes much more sense as it once again draws us directly to the cost that Jesus paid for us. They truly beat His body so badly that the evidence suggests He was unrecognizable as a man. His physical body suffered much in those last hours. He paid dearly for our salvation.

Statement #4: "My God, My God, why have You forsaken Me?" Mark 15:34

It is doubtful that any of us will ever be able to understand this cost that involves the Trinity. The Father, Son, and Holy Spirit had been in harmony forever. There had never been separation on any level at all. Now on the cross, the Son of God took upon Himself the sin of the world. What does all of this mean?

Several things occurred here. One, there was darkness. Scripture does not give any reason for the purpose of the darkness, but there seems to be some connection between the sin being placed on Jesus and His subsequent separation from the Father. Can you imagine all of the sin of the world dumped on the Son of God? Your sin. Our sin. The sins since creation. Rapes, murders, incest, adulteries, witchcraft, and so much more. He bore the sins of the world, and creation hid its Creator. Somewhere at the end of the three hours of darkness, Jesus spoke His fourth statement. Interestingly, He called God "My God." Jesus as Deity does not have a God, but as a man, He does. Was this the human Jesus speaking out? Was there separation in the Trinity that has never existed before? What all happened here? As best as we can understand, some kind of deep separation and agony occurred that only Deity would comprehend. This displays more of the cost of our Savior to us.

Statement #5: "I thirst." John 19:28

Cost can come in all kinds of shapes and sizes. Jesus' humanity was dehydrated, His mouth as dry as a potsherd. He struggled to speak. Out of the suffering came the words "I thirst." Yet another example of the cost He paid for us.

Statement #6: "It is finished." John 19:30

What was finished? The work the Father had sent Him to do came at a great price, not with silver or gold but with His precious blood (1 Pet. 1:18).

He paid an amazing price for the penalty for our sin. Are we truly able to grasp the depth of that cost?

> *Statement #7: "Father, into your hands I commit My Spirit."*
> *Luke 23:46*

He breathed His final breath. He had completed the work. He had finished well. It was now time to go back to the Father. He paid the full price. He paid the full cost. He paid for it all with His life. The hour came, and He met all the demands of the Father. His time to return home had come.

It is hard for us to grasp the depth of pain and agony that our Savior experienced in His last hours on this earth. Hell and the enemy unleashed their venom on Him, and He paid the tremendous cost because of His love for us. Scripture has likely not given us the depth of this cost. What has been included is certainly enough to prove that Jesus paid an incredible cost in just His last hours on this earth. How sad it is that few of His followers today are even willing to pay a small cost to stand up for Him and be accounted as His.

There is a rather powerful scene in *Les Miserables* by Victor Hugo that shows the cost the French revolutionaries were willing to pay. These men were willing to give their lives for an earthly goal. In the play version of the book, Enjolras speaks to Marius in one of the songs. As Enjolras speaks to a group of followers to drum up support, Marius is listening, but he is distracted by love. Enjolras berates him for it, telling him that he has a "higher call," a "larger goal," and that nothing is as important as that goal is; in fact, "Our little lives don't count at all."[2] *Our* goal, however, is so much more important than any earthly passion, and our lives count a great deal. We are talking about the Gospel and eternity and the glory of the Lord. Somewhere along the way, we must learn the lesson of those who went before us. There is a higher call. If we are about the Father's business, our lives are very important indeed. We have a choice to give Him our lives now by losing them or hold on to our lives now and lose them later. We are going to lose our lives one way or another. But let's keep this clearly in view: a life of cost is a meaningful life, and one worth living. The joy of serving the Lord overwhelmingly surpasses any cost we may ever pay.

2. Redmayne & Tviet. "ABC Cafe / Red and Black." *Les Miserables: The Motion Picture Soundtrack.*

TAKING THE CHAPTER A BIT FURTHER

1. Why was it necessary for Jesus to die, and what does that have to do with you personally?
2. Why did God also require Him to suffer so much? Wasn't His death atonement enough?
3. When He cries out on the cross and asks God why He was forsaken, what does that mean? Did God really abandon His Son? Will He ever forsake you?
4. How is it possible for Jesus, who is God, to die?
5. We know that Jesus rose from the dead. Why is this so significant?

Chapter 4

Jesus' First Followers Paid the Cost

On Sunday, January 26, 2020, the sports world suffered a horrific tragedy. Kobe Bryant, one of the greatest basketball players of all time, was killed, along with his daughter and several others, in a tragic helicopter crash. Needless to say, the basketball community and much of the world were in shock. Although accidents do happen, we often don't hear of one as tragic and somewhat avoidable as this seemed to be. Our hearts truly go out to Mrs. Bryant and her family, as well as the other families who suffered such great loss. Now, many people do not know the personal life of this man. We know of him, but do we really know who this man was?

Eventually, one person appeared on the sports channel, claiming to have great inside information on Bryant. The writer said he had known Bryant since childhood and had been with that family for many important seasons of their lives. It appears that this writer told the truth. Now, if you wanted to truly know the real Kobe Bryant, that particular writer's story might seem to be one worth reading. He could even give context to rumors that periodically circulated and explain which ones were credible. In theory, his story could take us so close to Bryant's life that we would think we were right there with him.

That kind of "insider scoop" is exactly what we have with the apostles. Not only are we given eyewitness accounts, but we also have the precious Holy Spirit, who promised to bring the specifics of Jesus' teachings back to each author. When we read Acts and the Epistles, we receive an exact amplification of what Jesus said and meant. As we read their historical writings, we are reading Jesus. Unsurprisingly, they use exactly the same force and emphasis Jesus did when they talk about the cost of following. Simply stated, if you are going to follow Jesus, it will cost you.

JOHN THE BAPTIST (JESUS' FORERUNNER)

Before we look at the first disciples, we should take some time to just examine John the Baptist. He was called the forerunner of Jesus, and he prepared for His way and arrival. John was the one who pointed out that Jesus was the Lamb of God who takes away our sin.

That picture of the Lamb first began in the Old Testament and appeared all throughout it from the very beginning. When God killed an animal and clothed Adam and Eve, what animal do you think He chose? Think also about the following examples: when Abel offered a more excellent sacrifice than Cain; when Noah offered his offering after the flood; when Abraham was about to kill Isaac and God had an animal already prepared (a ram caught by the horns so there was no blemish); when God's people offered an animal in Egypt and put its blood on the door; when the sacrificial system was put in place for Israel; when Isaiah spoke of an animal in Isaiah 53; and when John the Baptist arrived on the scene in the New Testament and called Jesus an animal. The animal in all those scenarios was the Lamb. All of them were pictures of the sacrifice that God would make of His Son on the cross. Jesus was that Lamb, that Passover Lamb, who takes away the sin of the world. And John the Baptist pointed Him out first.

But it is John's life that causes us to pause here, because he paid a great price to be the forerunner. Eventually, that calling led him to his death at the hands of Herod. Yet we need to keep in mind that John died long before he was killed. John died when he made the decision to be Jesus' forerunner; he died to himself before he died physically. Just listen to a few things that he said:

1. "I am the voice of one crying in the wilderness, make straight the way of the Lord." (John 1:23, KJV)
2. John saw his proper position in Christ when he said, "Whose sandal strap I am not worthy to loose." (John 1:27
3. He also described Jesus as "A Man who is preferred before me." (John 1:30)
4. "A man can receive nothing unless it has been given him from Heaven." (John 3:27)

5. "I am not the Christ, but I have been sent before Him." (John 3:28)
6. John only saw himself as "The friend of the bridegroom." (John 3:29)
7. "He must increase, but I must decrease." (John 3:30)

It is that last phrase that truly has gained the most attention. John makes it clear that life is not about himself. As a matter of fact, life is only about Jesus. It is our life's call to exalt Him and Him alone. Eventually, this calling cost John his life as he was killed by Herod for preaching the truth. There is a cost to following Jesus. John was the first example in the New Testament, but once Jesus began to preach and make disciples, that number grew. It was very evident from the day they chose to follow that being connected to Jesus would have an earthly cost. How have we moved from that truth?

THE 12 APOSTLES

The story of the apostles is absolutely riveting. Jesus took simple men from all walks of life and turned the world upside down. These disciples were fishermen, tax collectors, and as best we can discern, just normal people. Jesus called these men to follow Him, and they did to the very end. What happened to these 12 is not absolutely clear. We know of Judas who hung himself and of James who was beheaded. We know that John was exiled, and Peter would soon die according to the end of the Gospel of John. We also know that Paul—not one of the twelve—was near death according to 2 Timothy. Outside of that, we have to lean on tradition. So how can we be certain these stories are true? Thankfully, all the stories that have been passed down to us give the same information. In addition, the teachings of the New Testament assert that life would be difficult for these apostles throughout their ministry. So it's likely that traditions are not far off from the truth.

Here's what we learn from these traditions. Peter was crucified upside down because he did not count himself worthy to die the same way Jesus did. Andrew and Paul were also crucified. Thomas was pierced through with the spears of four soldiers. Philip was arrested and cruelly put to death. Matthew was stabbed to death. Bartholomew died as a martyr. James was stoned and then clubbed to death. Simon the Zealot was killed. Matthias, who took Judas' place, was burned alive. John was exiled, and some say he may have been put in boiling oil. Again, please keep in mind that these may be myths. However, there are *no* stories that suggest any other ideas, so on the surface at least, it would appear as if these stories are actually credible.

Why do we assume they are credible? The early church revered these men and certainly would have gone to great lengths to protect their stories.

In addition, their Master had died for the cause. He had taught them about the cost. Seemingly, this would be the logical conclusion to their journey of following Jesus. It was all part of the cost of following.

THE BOOK OF ACTS OVERVIEW

Another reason that makes me believe the stories of the martyrdom of the apostles is the writing of the book of Acts. Luke, the historian doctor who wrote the Gospel of Luke, gave us an amazing, detailed document about the first 30 years after the death of Christ. In Luke 1:1–3, he describes himself as one who was determined to accurately portray the historicity of his writings. He, not being an apostle, might have believed it necessary to affirm his credibility. The Gospel of Luke certainly lines up with the other writings of Matthew, Mark, and John. Although his work has material none of the others have, it does not contain anything that contradicts them. His writings come with much authenticity.

In Appendix 2, you can find a full listing of the verses in Acts that describe in some form or another part of the cost paid by the early followers of Jesus. Some examples are blatant and obvious, while others are more subtle. Put together, these form a clear picture of the cost many, if not all, of the early church suffered simply because they were followers of Jesus. Let me give you a few observations to solidify that thought in your mind:

1. Every chapter in Acts mentions the cost.
2. Overall, there are at least 112 different statements. Some describe the same event but in a different verse.
3. Throughout the Book of Acts, Luke has also interspersed much of Jesus' own personal suffering. Again, I suspect that it is part of the effort to keep the sufferings in the forefront of the followers as a reminder of who they are following.
4. There are at least eight named men who suffered a cost for following: Peter, John, Paul, Sosthenes, Gaius, Aristarchus, James, and Stephen. Of course, two of the people in this list suffered the ultimate cost by giving their lives: James and Stephen.
5. There are two key verses in Acts that may actually give us insight into the mindset of the early followers. Although both were written by the Apostle Paul, these two verses seem to capture their thinking rather precisely.

a. Acts 20:23–24—"except that the Holy Spirit testifies in every city, saying that chains and tribulations await me. But none of these things move me; nor do I count my life dear to myself, so that I may finish my race with joy, and the ministry which I received from the Lord Jesus, to testify to the gospel of the grace of God."

b. Acts 21:13—"Then Paul answered, 'What do you mean by weeping and breaking my heart? For I am ready not only to be bound, but also to die at Jerusalem for the name of the Lord Jesus.'"

6. Here is a sampling of some of the things that the early followers experienced.

   a. Scripture notes at least six different examples of beatings they suffered for following Christ.

   b. They were in prison eight times, but of course, God often broke them out.

   c. They were threatened some 11 times, and we know that these were not just warnings.

   d. False witnesses accused them 11 times.

   e. People attempted to kill them on 15 different occasions.

   f. They were chained twice, but added to the eight prison times mentioned above, it was probably closer to ten.

   g. On three different occasions, they were forced to flee a city.

One would have to admit that this is quite the list. They were beaten, threatened, imprisoned, and of course, martyred. Yet, the one thing that amazes me the most is what they did not do through all of this. If you read Acts carefully, you will not find one example of complaining, whining, being confused, doubting or questioning God, or crying from bitterness. How were they able to take this cost so well? Simply stated, they knew what they had signed up for. When they got out of the boat and left their nets, they might not have fully known all that was to follow, but after listening to Jesus' teachings, they certainly did. They counted the cost and stayed in the fight.

To follow meant that they might lose their lives. On several occasions they even said that they were ready. Are any of us ready to truly die for our faith? No one can be sure until that time comes, but these men all did. It is similar to the idea that you cannot kill that which is already dead. These men followed Jesus as dead men walking. They were dead, and their lives were hidden in Christ in God. You cannot kill a dead man. This reminds me of the words of Jim Elliott who wrote in his journal: "He is no fool who gives what he cannot keep to gain what he cannot lose."

Jim Elliott and his fellow missionaries died for Jesus spiritually before they ever reached the people of Ecuador. The apostles died with Christ and were raised to serve Him fully when they chose to follow Him. They did not count their lives dear to themselves. Today, far too many who call themselves followers have never died to self. Self is still on the throne of their lives, and the cost has not come into view. It is what happens when followers reinvent their Leader.

THE BOOK OF ACTS SPECIFICS

At the beginning of the book of Acts, the apostles are with Jesus, preparing for His return to the Father. He had already commissioned them in Matthew 28, but He does so again in Acts 1:8. This verse sets up the outline for the entire book. They started out in Jerusalem, then Judea, then Samaria, and then the entire world. By the end of Acts, the Gospel was all the way to Rome.

But how did it get to Rome from Jerusalem? Early on, it seemed as if they didn't want to go far from Jerusalem. As a matter of fact, in Acts 1–7, they were in Jerusalem and did not appear to be following the command of Christ to go. Acts 1:4 explains that they were told to tarry in Jerusalem until the Spirit came upon them. That occurs in Acts 2, so it would seem like the departure out of Jerusalem would begin right after that chapter. Acts 3:1 finds Peter and John going to the temple in Jerusalem. In Acts 4:1 they were still there. They were at Solomon's porch in Acts 5:11, which is still in the same city. Acts 5:42 says they were preaching and teaching daily in the temple. The number of disciples was multiplying in Jerusalem according to Acts 6:7. Stephen was brought before the council in Acts 7, which is also still in Jerusalem. I am not sure how many years passed in this time, but the apostles showed no signs of leaving. Maybe it was part of establishing the church at Jerusalem to be the base. Maybe they struggled to leave the confines of their homes.

Regardless of the reason, Acts 8 introduces persecution to the followers on a more intense level. There had already been some before this time, but Acts 8 introduces us to Saul (who later became the Apostle Paul). This man would set up the rallying cry to set off church persecution in Jerusalem. Acts 8:1 says that this great persecution at the Jerusalem church was the catalyst that scattered them abroad throughout the regions of Judea and Samaria (just as Acts 1:8 predicted). What did it take for that to happen?

Persecution. The church was now about to pay a severe, but necessary, price for following because it is costly to follow.

From this point on, in Acts we hear more about the Apostle Paul than any other. The other apostles traveled all over the world. The Gospel moved forward. As the apostles went, many paid the ultimate price. They paid the cost with their lives. Now let's pause here and think about the cost they and others paid for the Gospel. They were willing to pay a great price, but as Paul said often, he counted it all joy to suffer for Christ. He understood that any price he would pay would be far outweighed in blessings such as being more like Christ, being more used of Christ, being one day rewarded by Christ.

THE EXAMPLE OF PAUL

Although Paul was not part of the original chosen 12, he became an apostle by Jesus' later call on his life. This is actually rather interesting when you think about it. In Acts 1, when they tried to find a replacement for Judas based on Psalm 109:8, only two men met the criteria. Out of the two, they chose Matthias. The criteria were very specific; the man they chose needed to have been with Christ during His ministry and also a witness of the resurrection (Acts 1:21–22). Later, Paul called himself an apostle (Col. 1:1). How is that possible?

In 1 Corinthians 15:8, Paul mentions that Jesus appeared to him, as one born out of due time. Paul was suggesting that since he came to faith later, after Christ left the earth, he was not able to fulfill the original standards. In Galatians 1, Paul clarifies it further by talking about how he had received the teachings of Christ by revelation, not by human input. He was in the desert of Arabia for three years, and there Christ actually did meet and disciple him so that he truly met the standards of an apostle. Paul often had to defend that he was a true apostle because others questioned his qualifications. Nevertheless, he calls himself an apostle under the inspiration of the Holy Spirit at least 23 times. Regardless of how he became an apostle, Paul is clearly confirmed by Scripture to be one. As an apostle, he suffered the most of any of them and was more than willing to pay the cost.

He was even told that suffering would be a major part of his life. In Acts 9:16, right after Paul's conversion, God explains all the sufferings that will come Paul's way. Now, can you imagine after coming to faith in Christ, you are given this picture of the future? I cannot even fathom how that would work in our present world of comfortable Jesus. Can you imagine attending an evangelistic crusade preaching that theme? Or some of our churches preaching it? But, as Paul says later, none of those things moved him. Also, in Acts 21:11–13 he is reminded again of the future pain for following Christ. He truly received much at the hand of the enemy.

Here are my thoughts. We can maybe justify Paul having a severe price to pay because God said he was going to suffer for following Jesus. We also know that following during that time period came with an intense price to pay. Yet, Scripture mentions in numerous other places that there is a price to pay for following Christ. Maybe not all who follow will pay the identical price, but does it not seem that Scripture teaches it is costly to follow Christ regardless of time or era? Why are many of us so unwilling to pay any price? Is it possible we have so redefined Jesus that the Jesus we follow does not cost like the One in the New Testament? We'll examine more on that later, but let's look closely at Paul's cost he paid throughout the book of Acts.

In Acts, Paul describes the cost for following Jesus in at least 22 different verses or passages. Reading over these passages carefully gives one a fairly clear picture of the price he paid. Let me list them here for you so you can see the breadth of this cost. Some may be a simple comment. Some may be about the suffering that he experienced. Regardless, these verses show to some degree the cost he paid:

1. Acts 9:23—Threatened while in Damascus (just hours after his conversion)
2. Acts 9:29—Threatened again
3. Acts 13:50—Persecuted and ran out of Antioch
4. Acts 14:5—Faced possible stoning in Iconium
5. Acts 14:19—Stoned and left for dead in Lystra
6. Acts 15:11—Opposed and made the center of a controversy
7. Acts 16:23—Beaten with rods and imprisoned at Philippi
8. Acts 16:39—Cast out of Philippi
9. Acts 17:5–10—Threatened in Thessalonica
10. Acts 17:23–24—Forced out of Berea
11. Acts 17:18—Mocked in Athens
12. Acts 18:12—Taken before the judgment seat in Corinth
13. Acts 19:23–41—Opposed by the silversmiths in Ephesus
14. Acts 20:3—Plotted against by the Jews in Greece
15. Acts 21:27–30—Apprehended by the mob in Jerusalem
16. Acts 22:24—Arrested and detained by the Romans

17. Acts 22:24–29—Barely escaped being scourged
18. Acts 23:1–8—Rescued from the Sanhedrin mob
19. Acts 23:12–22—Avoided assassination plot against him
20. Acts 23:33–27:2—Imprisoned for two years in Caesarea
21. Acts 27:41–28:1—Shipwrecked on the island of Malta as he was being transported as a prisoner
22. Acts 28:13–15—Imprisoned in Rome, the first of several occurrences

And Paul's sufferings didn't stop there; you can read about Paul's cost throughout his writings. Let's look at a few examples.

In 1 Corinthians 15:30–32 he mentions that he fought with wild beasts while at Ephesus. Now, as best as we can discern, this is not a reference to actual beasts, but instead were people Paul faced who acted like wild animals as they opposed him. Later, in 2 Corinthians 4:17–18 he talks about always bearing in his body the death of the Lord Jesus. Paul was the first "dead man walking" in the Bible. But this is the call of all who follow Jesus! Also, in 2 Corinthians 6:4–5, he gives a brief list of some of his costs: afflictions, distresses, stripes, imprisonments, tumults, labors, and watchings. I'm not sure what all of those imply, but they appear to be part of the cost he paid willingly.

He also adds the word *persecution* in 2 Corinthians 12:10, Galatians 5:11, and 2 Timothy 3:10–11. Then, in 2 Timothy 4:6–8, he closes out his last Scriptural book by saying he had finished well. He knew he was about to die. But Paul was already dead. He had died long ago to Paul and Paul's dreams and Paul's will. He was sold out and surrendered and had become a bought vessel of the Lord's. He understood the call on his life.

The most intensive passage regarding Paul's cost is found in 2 Corinthians 11:23–28. In this passage Paul mentions at least 24 different components of the cost he experienced for following Christ. Due to the seriousness of this section, it is best to put it here in its entirety for us to observe carefully:

> Are they ministers of Christ?—I speak as a fool—I *am* more: in labors more abundant, in stripes above measure, in prisons more frequently, in deaths often. From the Jews five times I received forty *stripes* minus one. Three times I was beaten with rods; once I was stoned; three times I was shipwrecked; a night and a day I have been in the deep; *in* journeys often, *in* perils of waters, *in* perils of robbers, *in* perils of *my own* countrymen, *in* perils of the Gentiles, *in* perils in the city, *in* perils in the wilderness, *in* perils in the sea, *in* perils among false brethren; in weariness and

> toil, in sleeplessness often, in hunger and thirst, in fastings often, in cold and nakedness— besides the other things, what comes upon me daily: my deep concern for all the churches.

What a list. Some of these are not even recorded for us in the New Testament, which seems to suggest that maybe Paul's suffering was far worse than we can even imagine. Plus, there are several things that are open-ended in the passage, such as phrases like *more abundant*, *more frequently*, *often*, *perils*, *what comes upon me daily*, and *my deep concern*.

It is believed that Paul's conversion occurred in 36 AD and his death in Rome around 68 AD. If this is true, that would indicate a ministry of some 32 years. Since 2 Corinthians was written around 57 AD, this passage would only include the first 21 or so years of Paul's ministry. That would leave another 11 years of his life and work. Thus, Paul's list in 2 Corinthians 11 does not even cover all that he paid for the price to follow Jesus.

The cost to follow Jesus was taught by Him and lived by those who were closest to Him while He was on earth. They realized the cost and paid it, oftentimes paying the ultimate price as they were martyred. Yet, do we hear whining, complaining, and murmuring against God for these costs? Instead, we hear once again the praise for the privilege to be counted worthy to suffer for Christ. Here, in our no cost Jesus era, God's people are often grumbling and complaining while paying so little cost to follow. Maybe we are getting what we ask for by choosing a soft Jesus and our desire to make this world about self instead of His Kingdom.

TAKING THE CHAPTER A BIT FURTHER

1. How much of the cost did the early followers understand?
2. At some point in their individual faith journeys, the disciples realized that following Jesus required a great cost, yet they still followed him. Apply this to your own faith journey.
3. Why was Paul chosen to suffer as he did?
4. Are there any passages where one of His followers hints at struggling in their suffering for Christ? What does that teach us about our own suffering?

Chapter 5

The New Testament Epistles Taught There Would Be a Cost

The New Testament Epistles comprise the writings of six different authors. These authors are Paul (13 Epistles), Peter (2 Epistles), John (3 Epistles and Revelation), Jude, James, and the author of Hebrews. From these five or six men, we are able to extract the same message that Jesus taught while He was here on the earth. So, the pattern continues. Jesus taught it. The early church lived it. The final writers of the New Testament confirmed it by repeating the same principles as from the lips of Jesus. Since this pattern cannot be a coincidence, why don't we see this cost repeated in the lives of His followers today? Either we have misinterpreted the words of Jesus, or we have reinvented Him today in our personal view. You will have to decide for yourselves.

OVERVIEW OF THE EPISTLES ON THE THEME OF THE COST

To prepare for this study, I needed to read the Epistles carefully and attempt to highlight all the passages that pertain to this theme. This study helped me understand what the authors were trying to say, and I'm presenting the results here in case there are others who may be struggling. Here are a few things I discovered.

1. The issue of cost is recorded by every New Testament epistle writer, including the writer of Hebrews. All six authors believed it important enough to include it in some fashion or another. Some were more definitive than others, but all taught the same truth. These men not only lived the cost but also made sure that what they had been taught would be available for us to also learn and discern God's heart on this subject.
2. The theme can also be found in every book except 2 and 3 John. Now, these two books have very few verses (13 and 14 respectively) and cover only a few themes overall. However, the author, John, did discuss the cost in his other writings, so the theme is still presented by every author.
3. Some of the statements by the authors are not as clear as others. This pattern is the same with Jesus' teachings. In some passages Jesus makes it rather obvious, and in others, not so much. The same holds true for the rest of the New Testament. Again, how many times does an author have to say something in order for it to be true? According to God, only one time.
4. All of the five known authors use a certain title for themselves. (The author of Hebrews does not. I am not sure what that means overall; it may suggest that the author of Hebrews is really one of the other five.) The title that each of them uses is the title for servant. Some New Testament translators change it to *bondservant,* and some even prefer the word *slave*. Whatever you prefer does not change the heart of the teaching. We are not our own. We have been bought with a price. We are to lose our lives. We are to die to self. We are to not make this world about ourselves. Would these ideas not imply the concept of slavery? Here are a few quotes by some famous preachers:
   a. Alexander Maclaren—"The true passion, then, for a man is to be God's slave. . . Absolute submission, unconditional obedience, on the slave's part; and on the part of the Master complete ownership."
   b. Charles Spurgeon—"The early saints delighted to count themselves Christ's absolute property, bought by Him, owned by Him, and wholly at His disposal."
5. The Epistles have at least 77 different passages that deal in some way with the cost of following Jesus. You can find these in Appendix 3. Most of these are by Paul (not surprising, since he wrote most of the Epistles). Do you believe there is any other theme mentioned that many times in the Epistles?

6. The writers also make it clear that as we experience the cost of following Jesus in our suffering, we are partaking of Christ's suffering, and we are in some way enduring it with Him personally. This emphasis truly makes the cost a connection to our Savior and His teachings and life. Just look at how Peter described it in 1 Peter 2:21, 4:1, and 4:13. The last one is extremely clear as Peter says we are partakers of Christ's sufferings (1 Pet 4:13). How is this possible when Christ is already in Heaven? We are able to partake because part of the cost is following in His steps and being conformed to His image. If people hated Christ, they will hate us as well.

7. All through their writings, the writers allude to and give statements about the sufferings that Christ personally experienced. Just as Luke did in Acts, they also continuously kept the standard of Christ in the forefront. The early believers were to continue to remember the sufferings of Christ, His teachings about suffering for Him, and the ongoing examples of their fellow believers. If we are told to follow Jesus, then we need to be sure we are following the biblical Jesus and not some reinvented, soft Jesus.

8. The writer of Hebrews draws from the Old Testament to remind us that following God has never been easy. It is not some New Testament phenomenon but has always been part of a price God's children pay for being His followers. Just trace the history of Israel that is mentioned in Hebrews. Remember the first family and the cost Abel paid. Then, study carefully Hebrews 11, especially 11:33–38. In these verses we see the words *lions, fire, sword, weakness, fight, flight, tortured, cruel mockings, scourgings, bonds, imprisonment, stoned, sawn asunder, slain, wandering, destitute*, and *afflicted*. These costs paid by Old Testament followers mirrors the cost of the suffering of New Testament followers and those throughout church history. It is part of the call of being in this world but not of this world.

9. As you read through the Epistles, you will find it hard to discover one verse of complaining, murmuring, or questioning God. In the midst of paying the cost for following, these people were honored to be counted worthy to suffer for Christ. They counted the cost and were glad to pay the price. To them, He was worthy of that. That is the same theme found in 1 Peter 4:13 where Peter tells us to rejoice in that suffering and in Philippians 3:10 where Paul talks about the fellowship of Christ's suffering. Either these men and women were unique, or we have softened the call to follow.

INTRODUCTION TO THE EPISTLES

It would be daunting to attempt to study all 77 passages found in the Epistles about the cost. Instead, let's look at a few that clearly outline for us the importance of what it means to follow Christ. A deeper examination of even a few would be over the top for this study. So, the following will be a brief survey of these passages. You will discover that there is no soft follow or easy Jesus. This is a costly walk that will bring you to places and times that will cause your knees to buckle. Jesus taught and lived it. The early church understood, lived, and taught it. Now, will we live it?

Also, it is imperative to keep in mind that "cost" is defined by Jesus, not by ourselves. We may think we are paying a great price when in reality, we are not. Others may think that they are not, but our Lord sees it differently. The key is not to define the cost precisely. The key is to be willing to pay it. Again, keep in mind; what little we price we pay to follow Jesus is nothing compared to the glory that awaits us.

THE VERSES

Romans 12:1–3

These verses are foundational to this study. Paul reminds the readers to present their bodies (all that they have) to God. The idea is to give them to God and not take them back. We can argue whether this is salvation or sanctification, but the point remains the same. He is to have our all. Paul further develops that thought in the next verse by mentioning that we are not to be conformed to this world. The world is all about itself. It has to be because it is the unbelievers' only god. We are not to have this god before Him, who is the only true God. We are called to give Him our lives and not hold on to this world. We do that by being a living sacrifice. What a strange term. Doesn't the term *sacrifice* imply death? Yes and no. We are dead to ourselves, our lives, and our ambitions, and we are alive to Him and His plan and agenda. That is what Paul calls us to do. If for some reason we miss it in the first two verses, he clarifies it in verse 3. Don't think too highly of self. As a matter of fact, Jesus calls us to die to self. Today's culture tells us to build up, esteem, and put self first. "You deserve it," they tell us. No, my friends. We only deserve Hell, but by His grace, we have been given a chance to make a difference. Let's not let self interfere with that call.

Now, remember the flow of this passage. Romans 1–11 explains to us all that we have in light of the call to follow. We are saved, sanctified, justified, and so much more. As a result of all we have in Christ, Paul calls us to give the one thing back to Him that He wants from us, which is our lives. May we all desire to say, "God, I am yours." How often are you seeing that lived out in the daily Christian community?

Romans 14:7–8

These verses answer the whole issue about what is right or wrong for the believer to do. We are not our own. We don't live for ourselves, and we don't live to ourselves. We are His. He decides. He is Lord. He leads. He is our authority, and all that we have and do must flow through His will. If we live, we live for the Lord and His will. If we die, we die doing that will. Our life and will were given over to Him when we became living sacrifices on His altar. The only problem with many of us is that we tend to want to get back off the altar. Stay on the altar and live the life He has called for you.

Romans 15:3

There is more to this context, but let's just focus on verse 3, which reads, "For even Christ did not please Himself" (Rom. 15:3). That should be clear enough! We are to be followers of Christ and to live the Christian life as outlined by Him. Here is His call for us: do not live life to please self. Wow. Ever try that? When was the last time we lived like that? When was the last time we lived a day, a week, or a season like that? Today's believers are often so busy building their own kingdoms and agendas that there is little time to build His. Time to get out of the boat, leave the nets, take up the cross, and follow. That is the true following of Christ and paying the cost.

Romans 16:3–4

In these verses, Paul commends Priscilla and Aquila, his helpers in the ministry. Why? Because they risked their lives for him. The followers in this day understood from their Leader that following may cost them their lives. But that was not a great cost to pay since they had paid it long before the actual death would arrive. They paid it when they left the boats. They paid it when they left the tax collecting. They paid it by counting the cost and then following. We may never be asked to give our lives, but there is no question we are called to sacrifice our will and wants and wishes.

1 Corinthians 6:19–20

Here is another way Paul explains the verses from Romans 12:1–3. We can only properly understand that we are living sacrifices if we understand the truths of this passage. Our bodies belong to God. We are not our own, which makes it clear that we have no will, no rights, and no purpose outside of His call on our lives. He bought us with a price, and we know what that price was. It was the precious blood of Jesus (1 Peter 1:19). Value is often connected to what was paid to acquire something. He paid dearly for us, which gives us value. Then, we need to remember that since He bought us, He owns us. Period. No longer my will, but His be done. Do you serve as He has called you? Do you give as He called you?

1 Corinthians 7:23

Although this verse has so much more context to it, just notice the phrase included in the passage: "you are bought with a price." Paul had just stated that thought one chapter earlier as mentioned above. Yet, he thought it necessary to add it again already. He is trying to get his point across to a church body that was rapidly making life all about itself. Its members acted in such a way to fulfill their carnal desires and do as they pleased. Paul hits this thought hard throughout this book. It is as if he is saying, "You are not going to make a difference until you become a living sacrifice." As long as life is about you and your will, you are basically ineffective for His will. Maybe they needed a Garden of Gethsemane experience where they cried out, "Not my will, but Thine" (Luke 22:42).

Galatians 2:20

The heart of this verse is the same idea that has already been taught in Romans and Corinthians. This verse goes beyond the ideas of "living sacrifice" and "not our own" to make it so obvious we could hardly miss it. We have been crucified. I'm not sure what that means to you when you read it, so let's go back to our Leader, who was crucified. What happened to Him on that cross? He died. So, we have died also. We died when He died. We are not our own. In His grace He has given us life. Wow! What tremendous grace! As Jesus was raised, so we, too, have been raised to a new life—a life lived out in the presence of our Savior—a life that is truly only in Him and not about self.

Philippians 1:21

Paul continues with his theme, which we get the pleasure of seeing from one New Testament book to another. Here, it could not be any clearer. If we have any life at all, we have it in Christ as this verse states. As a matter of fact, to live is Christ. We are not our own. We only have life in the Son. We often see this as people's life verse. When do we see people living like that on a regular basis? How do our lives emulate this verse?

Colossians 2:20

Many believers know Galatians 2:20 but have missed Colossians 2:20. The context for this passage is being dead to the things of this world, such as what you can or cannot do. But at the heart of this premise is verse 20. Since we are dead with Christ, why are we living according to the world? Now, we all know what dead in Christ means, don't we? There was an actual death and resurrection; they both go together. In light of being dead with Christ, the only life we have is that life in Christ. We become dead to everything other than what He wants for us.

Colossians 3:1–3

Verse 1 builds off of what Paul said earlier in Colossians 2:20. While that verse talks about us being dead with Christ, Colossians 3:1 discusses being risen with Christ. That is the life mentioned in Galatians 2:20. We have been crucified, but we also live. Then, Paul further explains this truth to us in verses 1 and 2 by emphasizing the need to seek the things that are above. Set your affections on things above. In other words, live out the life that has been given to you since you died in Christ by living it entirely for Him. This is the living sacrifice idea. Yes, we have life, but it is not ours to live. Our duty is to sacrifice our lives daily for His will and His glory.

1 Thessalonians 3:1–4

There is so much to unpack in these verses, but we just want to focus on the major points. Paul was worried that the Thessalonians were struggling with their faith because of all the persecution they were facing. He was unable to be with them, so he sent Timothy to comfort them. He did not want them to falter over their suffering for the cause of Christ. They were paying the cost Jesus had talked about. Then, in verses 3 and 4, he reminds them of several critical truths. One, they were appointed to these things (v. 3), and two, when he was with them earlier, Paul had told them suffering would be coming (v. 4). Again, Paul simply reminds the followers of what Christ had said Himself: following Him would be costly. Does it cost us at all?

2 *Timothy 3:10–12*

Paul reports to Timothy his own personal persecutions and afflictions, which came on him while at Antioch, Iconium, and Lystra. These are all He recorded for us in Acts. Then, he offers great encouragement to Timothy of how God delivered him out of all of them. Verse 12 truly captures the heart of what Jesus taught and lived and what the early church understood: "Yea, and all that will live godly in Christ Jesus shall suffer persecution" (2 Tim. 3:12). In other words, if you live as Jesus taught, you will face opposition for following. You are going to pay a cost. When was the last time any of us paid a price for following? If this verse is a guarantee, then either we are not living godly, or we don't understand this verse. Yet, with the rest of the New Testament as a backing, does it not seem best to take this verse at face value?

2 *Timothy 4:6–7*

Paul wrote these verses near the end of his life. Most believe that Paul was about to die, and we have no recorded writings from Paul after 2 Timothy. It appears he was writing his own obituary. He declares in verse 6 that he is ready to be offered. Many other translations say this means being ready to be poured out as a drink offering. The idea is really deep in Old Testament theology where the sacrifice of a drink offering was part of the offering for the believers. Paul realized that the time of his departure from the earth was at hand. He was about to die. Most of us do not have the privilege of knowing when our lives will come to an end. Would it make any difference for us if we did? Paul makes this claim for his final days in verse 7: "I have fought a good fight. I have finished my course. I have kept the faith" (2 Tim. 4:7). In other words, "I have given my life to Christ, and I have finished well." Henceforth, a crown has been laid up for Paul and others who have run the race of life in the above manner. Paul was ready to lay his life down at the feet of Jesus. It was his worship, his offering, his way of saying, "Here is what I have done with my life. Are you pleased?" What if today was your last day? What would that offering look like? Have you lived this life for yourself or for His will?

These verses are simply a further explanation of Jesus' words. He stated clearly that following Him meant we would lose our lives. It meant loving Him more than anything. It meant we would carry our cross. Unfortunately, the church today has so reinvented Jesus that He does not look like the Jesus in the Gospels. He does not look like the Jesus described in Acts. He does not look like the Jesus who walked this earth and was seen of many. He does not look like the Jesus described in the Epistles. He looks like a Jesus that is soft, weak, timid, and comfortable. A Jesus that is here to give us a great life with no cost. A Jesus that is here to help us avoid persecution and suffering. A Jesus who is preparing a place for us in Heaven but requiring no sacrifice while we live on this earth. This Jesus is the modern Jesus who wants our lives to be so amazing, with no pain and no cost, that we will hardly think Heaven is a promotion. No wonder Jesus said that following him was a narrow way, and few would find it.

TAKING THE CHAPTER A BIT FURTHER

1. Why do you think it was important for the Epistles to reiterate much of what Jesus taught on the subject of cost?
2. What verses in the Epistles discuss the joy and privilege that they discovered in paying this cost?
3. How does living a life of cost cause greater blessing than defeat according to the Epistles?

Chapter 6

The Historical Church Has Paid the Cost

THE HISTORICAL COST TO THE CHURCH

It has long been verified that the church after the New Testament had a difficult and troublesome history of martyrdom, suffering, and pain—all for simply following Jesus. Following Jesus has rarely, if ever, been easy. Sometimes, the persecution is more severe than others, but it seems safe to say that during the time from the end of the New Testament to our present generation, the church has been riddled with pain. Numerous books have chronicled the suffering of God's people for the cause of Christ. Let's look at some of this pain and the lessons that follow from it.

Simply stated, Jesus taught that those who follow Him would pay a price. He taught and lived it. The early church experienced it. The Epistles expand on it in numerous passages. We should not be surprised to see this suffering continue after the writing of the New Testament. Yet we seem to think that we have entered an era where this no longer applies.

That perception, however, reflects a fairly insulated life that we in the West have experienced. The history of the church, from its inception and up through the present, is rife with persecution. Since the first apostles, people have been "beaten, ridiculed, defrocked, and defamed. They have suffered poverty, isolation, betrayal, and disgrace. They have been hounded, harassed, and murdered" according to George Grant of Ligonier Ministries.[1]

1. Grant. "A History of Persecution." *Tabletalk*, Ligonier Ministries, 1 August 2015.

Tertullian, writing in the third century AD, stated "The blood of the martyrs is the seed of the church." His quote contains both a shocking reality and a startling hope: where there is violent persecution, the church has grown and thrived. Yes, paying a price is costly. But the personal benefits and the Kingdom benefits far outweigh the price. Many of God's followers have counted it an honor to suffer for His Kingdom!

It is not just the early church that suffered. *Christian Today* writer Cath Martin relates that the number of believers martyred since the time of Christ is 70 million; among these, Nazi Germany killed approximately one million, and from 1917 to 1950, Russia recorded 15 million deaths.[2] Now, this just addresses the *deaths* of the followers of Christ! It doesn't include those who were injured, turned out of their homes, lost their jobs, and ripped away from their families. It also does not include those who were imprisoned, threatened, chased out of towns, or had their churches and possessions burned. Yet, even in spite of all this extremely painful persecution, the church has continued to grow and blossom. Maybe Tertullian's idea is consistent with the entire picture of the growth of the church.

This cost the historical church paid has provided a legacy for us, giving us the message of Christ. God's people died paving the way for us to have the words of Scripture, great hymns of the faith, teachings of depth, and stories of remaining faithful in the midst of the storms. Just as the Old Testament records examples for us, so also does the church of the past 2,000 years.

But with that solid legacy comes a sobering thought: if the Lord tarries, what will the generations following American Christianity say about us? In a country where we have had the opportunity to advance the cause of the gospel without resistance for many years, will it be said that we loved our cars, our homes, and our soft lifestyle as we sat in comfortable houses and churches? A generation that could be advancing the Gospel like no other may just go down as the generation that lost the opportunity. We simply did not want to pay the cost.

THE PRESENT COST TO THE CHURCH

Part of the problem for American Christians is that the cost of following Christ seems very foreign to us. We don't really take time to consider what is going on in the world. For example, think about the fact that the number of martyrs and those displaced and persecuted continues to rise worldwide. Here is one statistic: 900,000 Christians have been martyred in

2. Martin. "70 Million Christians Martyred." *Christian Today*, 25 June 2014.

the last decade, equating to 90,000 a year—one every six minutes.[3] Others are reporting similar numbers: "Credible research has reached the shocking conclusion that every year an estimate of more than 100,000 Christians are killed because of some relation to their faith," Vatican spokesman Archbishop Silvano Maria Tomasi announced in a radio address to the United Nations Human Rights Council in May 2020. Things sound pretty bad!

Yet in the U.S., the cost of following Jesus is either minimal or nonexistent. How have we escaped what the rest of the world seems to be experiencing on a regular basis? Our forefathers left the shores of Europe to come here for many reasons. One such reason was to escape religious persecution. As a result, they carefully included God's Word and the importance of religious freedom in our founding documents. Look at the first paragraphs of our Declaration of Independence affirmed on July 4, 1776:

> *The unanimous Declaration of the thirteen united States of America,* When in the Course of human events, it becomes necessary for one people to dissolve the political bands which have connected them with another, and to assume among the powers of the earth, the separate and equal station to which the Laws of Nature and of Nature's God entitle them, a decent respect to the opinions of mankind requires that they should declare the causes which impel them to the separation.
>
> We hold these truths to be self-evident, that all men are created equal, that they are endowed by their Creator with certain unalienable Rights, that among these are Life, Liberty and the pursuit of Happiness.

This document includes some very clearly-stated truths. The founders recognized the value of every human being, the potential for the government to do harm in tyranny, and the importance of freedom. Although it is rather lengthy, the ending of the Declaration sums it up well:

> In every stage of these Oppressions We have Petitioned for Redress in the most humble terms: Our repeated Petitions have been answered only by repeated injury. A Prince whose character is thus marked by every act which may define a Tyrant, is unfit to be the ruler of a free people.
>
> Nor have We been wanting in attentions to our Brittish brethren. We have warned them from time to time of attempts by their legislature to extend an unwarrantable jurisdiction over us. We have reminded them of the circumstances of our emigration and settlement here. We have appealed to their native justice

3. Walker. "900,000 Christians were 'Martyred.'" *Independent,* 13 Jan 2017.

> and magnanimity, and we have conjured them by the ties of our common kindred to disavow these usurpations, which would inevitably interrupt our connections and correspondence. They too have been deaf to the voice of justice and of consanguinity. We must, therefore, acquiesce in the necessity, which denounces our Separation, and hold them, as we hold the rest of mankind, Enemies in War, in Peace Friends.

Here, we see the colonists demanding the right to govern themselves and hearkening back to the "circumstances of our emigration and settlement here." Many of the colonists had left to escape religious persecution at home and to find a place where they could worship without the state telling them how. Some years later, the colonies created the Bill of Rights as an addition to the Constitution, approved on December 15, 1791. These rights were added to further detail some important standards learned from the years under British rule, particularly the danger of a too-powerful government. The first one, which guarantees religious freedoms, states: "Congress shall make no law respecting an establishment of religion, or prohibiting the free exercise thereof; or abridging the freedom of speech, or of the press; or the right of the people peaceably to assemble, and to petition the Government for a redress of grievances." The heritage of those who had fled religious persecution loomed large in the memories of the founders. They wanted to be sure that the government would have no right to interfere with their ability to worship God. The new government had many God-fearing men leading it, and for years to come, American Christianity was protected and spared of the atrocities in other parts of the world.

This protection has perhaps come with pitfalls. Undoubtedly, there have been seasons of amazing fruit from the church of America. We became the greatest country to send missionaries, the most magnanimous country, and so much more. God's people sacrificed and served and paid all kinds of costs to keep Him supreme in their lives and communities. God greatly used this time of calm to make a huge, worldwide impact. Yet as the years have progressed and we've become the most affluent country in the world, the depth of our faith has weakened and softened.

This time of calm has passed. The church in America is beginning to feel the effects of religious persecution. Some of the cost is easy to observe. The freedom to promote our faith is being greatly restricted on the educational campuses across the country. The Bible is clearly under attack. Church shootings seem to be a more regular occurrence. Those who voice their faith in public are ridiculed or shamed. Movies stars, politicians, athletes, and other high-profile people are mocked when they voice faith in God. Tim Tebow, a football player, may be one of the most obvious on this list. He won the Heisman trophy, the well-coveted award of college football athletes. He went on to have a limited pro career, but what was most noticeable was his outspoken faith. He knelt and prayed on the public arena and was vilified as the enemy of the people. *All that he did was kneel to pray.* He was not forcing it on anyone. He just did as his faith led him, and he was not trying to set an example for the rest of the world in doing so. People mocked him and told him to get his faith off the field. Colin Kaepernick, another football player, also knelt, but for a different reason. He knelt to promote his concern over social justice and set a precedent for others to follow. People espoused his cause and called him a hero. This is not an attempt to cast stones at either man, but to just get a high-level glimpse of society's current attitude toward Christianity. Tebow had his supporters, but he was largely "crucified" in the press and by social media. Kaepernick, by contrast, was honored. Now, there is always more to a story, but the bottom line is Tebow claimed to follow Jesus Christ. From an earthly view, this has cost him dearly.

Another example is the vice president of the United States, Mike Pence, who was in office during President Trump's tenure. Mr. Pence is an outspoken Christian, who often called on Americans to pray and trust the one true God. As a nation, at the time of this writing, we are going through a season of crisis. The coronavirus (COVID-19) has shut our country down. People are suffering worldwide, and many have died. Mr. Pence headed up that important task force to stop this dreadful disease. He called on our country to pray. Believe it or not, he has been mocked for this request. It is all part of the wave of persecution that is coming our way. The time of calm is coming to an end. We have had some years without persecution, but rarely does God's church avoid the perils of the cost of following Jesus. He taught it. He lived it. The apostles lived it. The early church lived it. The Epistles taught it. The church down throughout history has lived it. The lesson is just this: we must be prepared, because no matter how comfortable we want our Christianity to be, we, too, will live that persecution at some point. Is your faith ready?

TAKING THE CHAPTER A BIT FURTHER

1. What does the historical record of the suffering of God's people reveal to you regarding the cost today?
2. Study the early church and read the stories of the persecution. What effect did that persecution have on the church as a whole?
3. What do you think a cost for following Jesus would look like today? Does it have to require persecution?

Chapter 7

Important Principles for Interpreting Scripture Regarding the Cost

WE WOULD NOT HAVE different views of Jesus if there was not some problem in the interpretation process. There seems to be a disconnect between the words that appear in passages and their present-day interpretation. What happened to sever that connection between the historical Jesus and our interpretations of Scripture?

IS IT POSSIBLE TO TAKE JESUS HISTORICALLY AND LITERALLY?

So let's start with the basics. I believe that the Gospels recorded in the original manuscripts are accurate. I will not debate textual criticism. If you do not adhere to these historical and strongly accepted documents, then a different study may be for you.

For those who accept these Gospels as accurate, although we understand there are some minor problems, the rest of this study should prove helpful. If we are going to discuss the cost of following Jesus, we must correctly handle what He said.

True, many critics say we can't take Jesus' words literally. They use examples from various passages. For instance, Jesus said, "If your right eye offends you, pluck it out" (Matt 5:29), and "if your hand offends you, cut it off" (Matt 5:30). Rather extreme ideas are they not? Does anyone *really* believe Jesus meant this to be interpreted exactly as He said it—as in literally plucking out an eye or chopping off a hand? We all know that we don't need eyes to lust. Yet the critics want us to believe that if we cannot take everything Jesus said in the strictest of literal senses, then nothing should be examined as literal. That just is not accurate handling of the text.

There are other examples as well. Jesus said that He was the Door. Does anyone think that means a literal door? Jesus said He was the Vine (John 15:5). Does He mean to say when you look at a vine, treat it well because it is really Him? We understand that Jesus spoke at times using imagery that allowed the listener to better understand what He was saying. There is no evidence that Jesus intended literal interpretation in those cases. Also, right after that passage on chopping off your hand and plucking out your eye, Jesus taught about divorce. Many conservative scholars believe that we are to take Matthew 5:31–32 (on divorce) literally but not the verses before that which discuss cutting off a hand, etc. Who makes those kinds of decisions on interpretation? Is this not a dangerous path?

If anyone desires to handle the Word accurately, that person is going to need at least some standards of Bible interpretation so that the student does not become an end in himself. Bible study needs principles for accurate interpretation that limit imagination and reading into the text.

SOME KEY PRINCIPLES IN BIBLE STUDY

There needs to be some simple rules when interpreting the Bible to keep the person from concluding things based on his own bias. Here is why that guideline is important. For example, a person may look at Matthew 5:31–32, which says that you cannot marry another who has been divorced. If you do so, you are an adulterer. If that person has gone through a divorce for a reason other than what Jesus stated in the passage (immorality), they may conclude we should not take those verses literally. So, they become their own interpreter of Scripture and can justify divorce for almost any reason. Obviously, that is not a good approach to Scripture. That is part of our problem today with understanding Jesus. Those who want a lifestyle that does not involve much cost try to avoid taking Jesus' teachings literally. They rather neatly avoid the passages on cost that are pervasive in the Word of God.

Of course, it doesn't have to be this way. If we approach God with certain principles firmly in mind, our study of Scripture will be much more useful (and much less confusing).

Principle #1: All Scripture is given by God and is profitable.

It is important to keep in mind what God says about His Book. Paul, in writing to Timothy, explained that "All Scripture is given by inspiration of God and is profitable" (2 Tim. 3:16). Now, when Paul was writing this to Timothy, the only Scripture that was truly available would have been the Old Testament. Yet, when the Bible was later completed, the additional books of the New Testament were included in this inspired list. Therefore, all of Scripture is inspired by God, both the Old and New Testaments. Regardless of where you end up in your study of the words of Christ, you still have to conclude that these books are profitable.

Principle #2: No Scripture is of any private interpretation.

The Bible is very clear about this. 2 Peter 1:20–21 tells us that "no prophecy of Scripture is of any private interpretation, for prophecy never came by the will of man. . ." The word *prophecy* here refers to the Scriptures in general, not any specific prophecy. The point of the verse is that no one has an exclusive understanding of the Bible. God gave the Scriptures to the church for wise teachers and preachers to handle the text carefully. Yet, we all need to do our homework and know what it means. When we stand before the Lord, we cannot be shielded by someone's false teaching. We need to be students ourselves.

Therefore, it is your responsibility to take these passages that have been shared in this study and digest them under the guardianship of the Holy Spirit. You have been given one perspective so far. When the dust settles, you will give account of the accurate understanding of the text. That is why it is important that you study to show yourself approved unto God (2 Tim. 2:15).

Principle #3: When studying any passage, examine the whole of Scripture for confirmation of your interpretation.

Far too often we interpret a passage and stand on that passage alone as if our interpretation is accurate. If there are no other passages that support your interpretation of that Scripture, then you should take a few steps back for further clarity. One example of this can be found in John 13. Jesus washed the disciples' feet and discussed the importance of following His example. Now, we have two ways to look at that example from the Lord. One, we should actually wash each other's feet in some form of regular church life. Two, Jesus was teaching about humility and servanthood. While both can be construed in some ways, the idea of foot washing is something to be critically evaluated. When you examine the Epistles carefully, you will see no explanations on how this is to be done as there are teachings like baptism and communion. The lack of information is cause to wonder whether foot washing should be part of the church like baptism and communion. Washing feet can be something that has meaning, but is there enough clarity to make it a regular component of church life?

When studying Matthew through John, you must also examine the Epistles to see what insights are found to validate the teaching. It's not that Jesus' words need validation, but not all that He said was for us today. Some teachings were cultural for his time. For example, when Jesus sent out the disciples, He told them to only go to Israel. Why did He only send them to Israel? Because that is why He initially came. He came unto His own, and His own received Him not (John 1:12). Eventually, He had them turn to the Gentiles. But at first, His mission was clearly only for the Jews. Should we adopt that guideline as well and only go to the Jews?

Another important example is Jesus' view of the Sabbath. We know that the Jewish Sabbath was from Friday evening till Saturday evening, roughly beginning and ending at 6:00 p.m. Jesus was careful with the Sabbath day, and He even led His disciples to honor it as well, respecting the fourth commandment. However, few scholars today are of the impression that this Old Testament Sabbath is required in the same way for us today. The Epistles bear that out, as well.

So, when we are studying these truths, we must make sure to confirm our conclusions elsewhere in Scripture. Chapter 5 discusses that very premise. The interpretation of the cost of following Jesus can be clearly delineated in the Epistles. Scripture compared with Scripture bears out the conclusion for us. Paul taught it. John taught it. Peter taught it. James taught it. Jude taught it.The writer of Hebrews taught it. That is how you can confirm Biblical principles.

Principle #4: We have the Holy Spirit so we can discern the truth of Scripture.

We are not flying blindly here when studying Scripture. It is not as if we have no clue or chance of knowing the truth. The Holy Spirit was given to us at salvation to guide us into all truth. There is no need for us to be aimless. The truth is within our reach, and we need to seek it with a deep passion. Far too many believers are not even in the Word. How can we expect to discern the deep things of God when we only settle for minutes in His presence? God's Word is like a deep treasure that is available to us as we wait upon the Lord. We cannot expect to understand these truths without a passion for His truth and presence.

Maybe we need to ask the Holy Spirit to illuminate our hearts and minds as we wait upon the Lord in His presence. Maybe we need to be still in His presence and quit being distracted by the world so that the passion for Him and His Word can grow. It is like snacking all day and then having no appetite for dinner. We cannot gorge ourselves on the junk food of this life and world and then try to eat the hearty, nourishing food God provides. Or, to change the analogy a bit, whatever we feed is going to grow the most. Try it: feed your hunger for God, and watch it grow. Feed your patience in His presence, and watch Him guide you into all truth.

Remember that teaching that is not embedded in Scripture is simply man's opinions. If a study does not drive you to Scripture, then be wary. Study the best. Study the Word. When the Scripture shows you the cost, then live it.

Principle #5: If the plain sense makes sense, seek no other sense.

This thought was shared with me years ago when I was in Bible college. I'm not sure which professor gave that truth to me, but it has lasted and benefitted me for years. It is the best way to look at Scripture. There are several corollaries that proceed from this truth. For instance, don't assume that there are hidden truths and numbers and prophecies all throughout Scripture. It is not some kind of magic book. Additionally, don't assume that there are multiple meanings to every passage. Typically, each passage has just one meaning. Finally, don't assume that when someone comes up with a "deep" thought about a passage or series of passages, no one else has ever thought of it as well. For example, Proverbs has 31 chapters. Someone could conclude that the Holy Spirit inspired that number so we could have a chapter a day to match our calendar. Is that "deep" thought? Remember that verse breaks and chapter breaks are not part of inspiration but interpretation.

So, what do we do with this principle? When Jesus says to believe in the Lord Jesus Christ and be saved, we need to accept it for exactly what it is. It is not complicated. When Paul says that an elder needs to be not given to wine, there is no need to overstate that. It is what it is. Elders must stay sober-minded all the time so they have ample insight into truth and are not hindered by alcohol. They are to be on call at all times, so there is no room to have something controlling them other than the Person of the Holy Spirit. The plain sense needs to speak for itself. Stop trying to find hidden truths.

Now, we need to pause and think this principle through with the passages that we have already examined. Does God expect us to hate? Does God really want us to die? Does He want us to serve or be last or learn to give our life away? These cannot be taken literally, or can they? This is where the soft Jesus comes into play. We weaken the amazing teachings of Jesus and throw the "it can't mean that" cloth over it so as to put out the fire. We must apply this principle in these difficult passages.

The plain sense and literal sense are hard to distinguish at times. Literal sense would say if I die, I cannot live for him. However plain sense makes it clear what He is saying. We cannot live two lives; one for Him and one for me. The plain sense flows out of the literal. As we learn to die to self, we can then learn to live for Him.

Again, if the plain sense makes sense, seek no other sense. It is very sensible to believe that a Savior who gave His life up and offered Himself as a sacrifice would expect that of His followers. It also makes sense that we cannot serve both self and God. One has to die. It makes sense that the cost to follow Jesus would exist because the world hated Him, and He said it would hate us. Yes, there is a cost to follow, and it is revealed in the plain sense of His teachings. Let's watch how this works:

1. If we die to self, we are more able to serve Him fully.
2. If we give our lives away, we have less of a chance of self grabbing our hearts.
3. If we put ourselves last, we have more opportunities to put Him and others first.
4. If we serve, we will learn to put self last.

God does not need to make sense to us. When the text speaks, let it speak accurately and literally unless there is no possible way for it to be literal.

Principle #6: Scripture is the best interpreter of itself.

Many believers spend time on the websites of famous authors, podcasts, books, and other teachings by popular writers and speakers. These gifted men and women certainly have a place God has intended for them, but why should we spend hours in the presence of a mere human when we have access to God Almighty? Some believers are cheating themselves from the greatest Teacher ever. We need a fresh hunger for the Word in the presence of the Author. As a matter of fact, this is the only book that you need to know the Author personally and understand His writing. Do you know Him?

Please don't dismiss all the great writings that are out there. But again, none of them compare to the precious Word of God. Therefore, when you are studying a verse, a passage, a chapter, or a book of the Bible, remember that it is a Bible study. It is never a verse, passage, chapter or book study. It is always a Bible study. Going deeper in any one of the 66 books should also drive you way beyond that one book. How can one study the life of Christ and not look at the Old Testament and the Epistles? It is the same for any book of the Bible.

As you dive into the Word, you will find that Bible study is more rewarding. Have a good resource nearby that can suggest passages that are parallel to the one you are studying. As you do so, you will see the entire Bible open up. For example, when we study Matthew through John, we see many of His teachings revealed in the Epistles. These books help support Jesus' words and reveal the meaning of those words. Jesus meant for us to die. Just ask Paul. He planned for us to bear our cross. Just ask Peter. The cost is clearly taught all throughout the New Testament. To dismiss this truth is to dismiss not only Jesus' teachings but also the entire New Testament.

Principle #7: Not all of Jesus' commands are for us today.

One final thought is also important: not all of the commands that Jesus gave are truly commands He expects for us now. When Matthew ends his writing in chapter 28, he records several verses that have become known as the Great Commission; go into all the world and preach the Gospel. In these verses, Jesus gives some important details for His followers to move forward after His ascension: go into all the world and make disciples of all nations, teaching and baptizing the disciples. But there is one truth that is often overlooked in this last command of Jesus. It is the one where He states exactly what He wants His disciples to teach. He did not want the disciples to teach randomly or aimlessly. He gave to them the exact curriculum that they were to take with them and teach. He told them to teach everything He had commanded them. To further ensure that this would happen, He also gave them the Holy Spirit, who would bring back to their remembrance all of this teaching (John 14:26). What a plan He had! He taught them and gave them the Holy Spirit, who, with His omniscience, would have all the truth for them. Then, Jesus sent them out with a perfect plan to give to us the truth today. No need to worry if we have the Truth. God had a plan, and we can be sure we have His truth just as He wanted it to be.

Jesus commanded them to go out in pairs, shake dust off feet, raise the dead, and many other things. All of the commands given to them do not necessarily apply to us. So, how about the ones we are studying? Be sure the Epistles support any command you see. Use His word to confirm the directives.

What will you do with this? My prayer is that you will study once again the teachings of Jesus and begin to examine them for their plain and literal meaning. Then when you discover that He has said some amazing truths, then my prayer is that move you into living the life as He has explained is true of a follower of His.

TAKING THE CHAPTER A BIT FURTHER

1. Read one of the Gospel accounts and begin to notice passages where the sense of the text is hard to discover. Apply the above principles and see if you can discern the intent of the passage.
2. Read the book of Hebrews and notice all the Old Testament passages that are alluded to in that book. Research a few of those passages and see how the passages are connected. For example: in chapters 3 and 4, the writer of Hebrews uses the word "rest" and connects it to the wilderness wanderings. What is the rest in Hebrews and how is it similar to rest as described in the Old Testament? This process is how you interpret passages, by comparing the larger scope of Scripture.

Chapter 8

Exegesis of Some of the Key Passages Taught by Jesus About the Cost

OVER THE FIRST SEVEN chapters of this book, we've established that following Jesus comes with a cost. Keep in mind we are not talking about heart disease, cancer, car accidents, or other problems that nonbelievers share with us. We are talking about a direct cost that comes only to those who follow Jesus and attempt to live and express that faith. That is the kind of cost the New Testament clearly teaches.

With that foundation in place, let's go back to the teachings of Christ that we earlier glossed over and merely presented as our argument. These passages are also listed for us in Appendix 1. Chapter 1 gave the gist of His teachings, but now let's go back and examine some of these in more detail. As we've said, in order to avoid reinventing Jesus' teachings, we have to let His words speak for themselves. Did Jesus really mean what He said?

SOME OF THE KEY PASSAGES OF JESUS

Appendix 1 lists 73 different passages that directly teach the cost of following Jesus or allude to it in some way. A thorough study of all of these passages is not necessary. Taking a closer look at a few should be sufficient to make the point. I have chosen 10 to attempt to show the importance of this from Jesus' own teachings.

Again, we have to ask a simple question: how many times does Scripture have to say something in order for it to be true? When you examine the New Testament, including all 27 books, you will find that lessons about the cost of following Jesus appear at least 263 times! While some are strongest when used in conjunction with others, together they make a very definitive whole! Below are the passages we will examine:

1. Matthew 4:18–22—The original call to pay the price and follow
2. Matthew 6:19–33—The call to pay a price regarding our hearts
3. Matthew 10:1ff—The call to pay a price
4. Matthew 19:16–22—The call to pay a price with an example
5. Matthew 19:27–30—The call to pay a price as modeled by the apostles
6. Matthew 20:26–28—The call to pay a price as modeled by Jesus
7. Matthew 22:34–40—The call to pay a price by loving God with ALL
8. Luke 12:15–34—The call to pay a price to the things of the world
9. John 15:19–20—The call to pay a price and be hated by the world
10. John 21:15–17—The call to pay a price by loving not the world

It is my hope and prayer that these 10 passages will help you understand the Savior's call about what it truly means to follow Him. May we be hearers of His Word and doers. Now, let's dig deeper into the key passages that address this theme.

Matthew 4:18–22

Our first passage relates the call of the first apostles as recorded in the New Testament. At this time, it was not uncommon to find a teacher who had a group of followers. John the Baptist had his own disciples, and some of these later joined up with Jesus. Now, we do not know all the background to this passage. Were some of them followers of John? Had some already listened to or heard about Jesus? We are left with the basics of the text to determine the breadth.

Jesus was walking by the Sea of Galilee and saw two brothers casting a net into the water. Their names were Peter and Andrew. He called out to them, "Follow Me, and I will make you fishers of men" (Matt 4:19). Now, what exactly was Jesus saying to these men? Well, the answer to that question lies in how they responded. Matthew 4:20 says, "They immediately left their nets and followed Him." There is quite a bit inherent in that action.

Much like Americans did up until the middle of the last century, many young men in Jesus' time followed their dads into the family business. Therefore, to follow Jesus, Peter and Andrew would have had to leave their family, business, boats, nets, and futures. This decision was huge. We gloss over it today as if they just got out of their boats and served on weekends or in between fishing trips. Yet, if we read the gospels, it appears these men gave much more than that. When they got out of that boat, they said "goodbye" to everything. On that day, they died to self.

In that same passage, Jesus also calls James and John brothers from the fishing business. Matthew 4:22 says, "Immediately, they left the boat and their father, and followed Him." The text makes it clear—they left everything behind them. They even bring this up to Jesus later in His ministry (Matthew 19).

Do their actions prove that they understood the cost of what it meant to "leave" and follow? What exactly does the word "left" mean? In this case, their actions help define the word. They got out of the boat and put it in their rearview mirror. The actual word here is *aphiemi*, pronounced *af-ee'-ay-mee*. Since the word is found 146 times in the New Testament, we have ample data to determine what the verb means. It is the same one used for Peter and John when they left, and it also appears for John and James. It is such a strong word that it can also be translated as *forgive*. Jesus used it in the Lord's prayer when He said, "and forgive us our debts" (Matthew 6:12). Matthew mentions that word 47 times, and for 17 of those occurrences, he uses it to mean *forgive* or a word similar to that. Biblically, we know the meaning of the word *forgive*. Clearly, it signifies to let something go. Jesus even states that if we did not let go by forgiving, then our Father in heaven will not forgive us.

This word is also used by Matthew to describe the fever leaving Peter's mother-in-law. It left her so completely that she was immediately able to serve Jesus and the others. The passage seems to imply the fever left and never returned. This word is also used in Matthew 24 in reference to the Second Coming, when Jesus will return and take the remaining believers to inherit the Kingdom and remove the nonbelievers for judgment. ("One will be taken, and the other left" [Matt 20:40].) This example describes a departure with no return.

As best as we can tell from the New Testament, the next time the disciples returned to their nets was in John 21. It is here that Jesus asked Peter, "Do you love Me more than these?" (John 21:15). Could it not be a direct statement towards the initial departure from the nets? When Jesus had died, the disciples felt abandoned and alone. They did not know what else to do but go back to what they knew before Jesus, which was their nets. It appears that if they had truly understood the resurrection, they would never have returned to fishing. Getting out of that boat meant to never return to that lifestyle. Their lives as they knew it were over. Now, the only life they had was the one Jesus had given them.

Was that call for Peter, Andrew, and the others unique to them, or is it as serious a call for us today? To answer that, let's proceed to some more passages.

Matthew 6:19–33

This next passage is a section from the famous teaching of Jesus often called "The Sermon on the Mount." Jesus' teachings in Matthew 5–7 are some of the most poignant and powerful of all His words. He begins right at the start by stating what it means to follow Him. He leaves nothing to guesswork. If you follow, there is a cost to pay.

In this particular section of the sermon, He discusses the heart of the believer. It is probably best summarized in these verses. Matthew 6:21 says, "for where your treasure is there will your heart be also," and then Jesus declares, "No one can serve two masters" (6:24). Finally, Matthew 6:33 states, "But seek first the Kingdom of God." These verses address the rule of the heart. Who or what controls you? Who or what leads you? Whom or what are you living for?

From the very beginning, there has been a battle over the control of our hearts. Satan succeeded in pulling at Adam and Eve and encouraging them to go after what they wanted instead of following what God had commanded. That battle still rages in all of us, and it will keep on until we finally arrive home. Jesus is using the outward to expose the inward. Man can only see the outward, but God looks on the heart. It is the heart that controls the outward response. If our hearts are in the right place, then the rest of our lives will fall into place. There is no room to have two masters in our lives. That is why the first commandment reminds us to have no other gods before Him. He is to be the Supreme Ruler in our lives. That evidence can be seen by what it is that we seek. Find a person who seeks the things of the world, and you will find a person who does not have his heart in the right place. Find a person who is passionate about the call of Christ, and you will find a true follower. You will find a person who has counted the cost and is willing to pay it for the cause of His Savior.

Throughout this passage our Lord intersperses some amazing verses of encouragement for us. If we choose to live this way, God has reassured us that we won't starve or go without what we need. Jesus is making it clear that when we sell out to His call, the things that we need are surely to be available. Just think of it this way: we are taking none of this with us. So, why not invest in the eternal where moth nor rust destroys and where thieves cannot break through and steal? This passage is a call to examine our hearts. Does He have your heart, or does the world have it? You can answer that by examining your treasures. If your treasures are on this earth, you have not discovered the call to lose your life for His work. You are still putting your will first. You have your treasures in the wrong place. Does this describe you?

Matthew 10:1–29

This chapter begins innocuously enough. Matthew lists the apostles' names, beginning with Peter and ending with Judas. Jesus informs the disciples that they have been given power to do amazing miracles. Then, in verse 5 He sends them out.

He first gives them their focus. Jesus clearly came for the lost sheep of the house of Israel, and His disciples were being sent out with the same directive. Do not go to the Gentiles; rather, go to Israel. Preach as you travel, heal, and perform miracles. Don't even worry about your daily needs. Jesus explains that He will provide for them. He then explains what the disciples should expect; some people will receive them while others will reject them.

However, the words of verse 16 are really the ones that must have truly stirred their hearts. Here is just the first half of the verse: "Behold I send you out as sheep in the midst of wolves" (Matt 10:16). Now, I doubt we need much education on the clarity of that statement. Wolves chase, stalk, and kill sheep. They were in for trouble.

The rest of the passage bears out that claim as He states in several verses that they would not be sitting back in comfort. They were going to war. The following is a list of some of those statements:

1. Verse 17—". . . they will deliver you up to councils and scourge you . . ."
2. Verse 21—"brother will deliver up brother to death . . ."
3. Verse 22—"And you will be hated by all . . ."
4. Verse 23—"When they persecute you in this city, flee to another. . ."
5. Verse 24—"A disciple is not above his teacher . . ."
6. Verse 28—"And do not fear those who kill the body . . ."
7. Verse 29—". . . not one falls to the ground apart from your Father's will."

It does not take much imagination to see what Jesus is saying to those who follow Him. They will pay a great cost. Why do we believe there won't be one today?

Matthew 19:16–22

A rich young ruler wants to have eternal life. Jesus teaches him about cost. Was He misunderstanding the question? No, He just understood perfectly well what the young man was *really* asking. Jesus understood the rich young ruler's request was not simply about Heaven. He was asking how to become one of His disciples. Jesus answered his real request with an answer that hit at the heart of his problem, "If you want to be perfect, go, sell what you have and give to the poor, and you will have treasure in Heaven; and come, follow Me" (Matt 19:21).

Notice His last words: "follow Me." Jesus quickly explained to the man that Heaven and following Him were connected. In other words, no one can go to Heaven without following Him.

Unfortunately, many claim they will go to Heaven, and yet, there is no evidence of a personal faith and walk with Christ. How have we reached a place in our biblical thinking that we believe we can follow Christ in a way that is actually foreign to the teachings of Christ? Verse 22 shows that Jesus had hit the heart of the young ruler's problem. It wasn't "doing good things" that was his issue–it was the status of his heart. He wasn't truly willing to pay the cost, which meant committing himself fully to Jesus instead of to his "stuff." In fact, the text says that the rich young ruler "went away sorrowful because he had great possessions." Jesus asks us, "What does it profit a man to gain the whole world and lose his soul?" (Matt 16:26). Maybe affluent America needs to do some soul searching.

Matthew 19:27–30

It is one thing to *think* we understand what Jesus said, but it extends further when we see how those who heard what He said lived and interpreted His words. Passages such as this one give us pertinent insight into that search. Notice what Peter says to Jesus in verse 27: "Behold we have forsaken all, and followed thee; what shall we have therefore?" (Matt 19:27)

Although Peter used a different word than what was recorded in Luke 14:33 "forsake all," the word still means *to leave* or *forsake*. As a matter of fact, it is the same word used in Matthew 4 when the disciples were called, and they forsook their boats and nets. Jesus recognized the seriousness of

Peter's statement by then connecting it to following Him, saying, "you who have followed Me" (Matt 19:28). It is also important to note that Jesus did not correct Peter. He didn't say, "No, you have not forsaken all for my sake." Considering His comments to the rich young ruler, we can see that He probably would have taken His disciples to task if they had misspoken here. This implies that they did, indeed, understand the cost of following Jesus, at least up to this point in their lives.

In the rest of the passage, Jesus adds that whoever leaves houses, family, or land for His sake will not go unrewarded. If you pay the cost and end up last (as mentioned in verse 30), one day, you will be first. It is clear that we will lose our lives either way. We either lose it now for His call and gain it later, or we live life as we wish now and lose it later, in eternal separation from God.

Matthew 20:26–28

Let's start by reading this whole passage:

> *Yet it shall not be so among you: but whoever desires to become great among you, let him be your servant; And whoever desires to be first among you, let him be your slave, just as the Son of man did not come to be served, but to serve, and to give His life a ransom for many.* (Matt 20:26–28)

Verses 26–27 are rather straightforward. Die to self and your wants and put His call first in your life. Easy to discuss, but much harder to live. Paul later said we are to esteem others better than ourselves (Phil. 2:3). Our will continues to be a battlefield, and far too often our will wins. Living this kind of life is simply not easy, but Jesus never said it would be. We just have to come to grips with the fact that we have two choices on how to live this life: live it as we please and stand before Him one day only to find out we lost it all, or lose it all now for His call on our lives and stand before Him one day to receive our reward.

Now check out the latter part of the passage. Jesus uses His own example as the model in this journey of ours. He makes it clear that He did not come to be ministered to but to minister and give His life. We need to keep that verse in mind as we try to understand what Jesus is teaching. To put it rather simply, follow His example.

Don't you find it interesting that many of the religious leaders throughout history have often made it about themselves? For example, don't you find it disturbing that those who want their followers to strap bombs to their bodies and die as martyrs are not willing to do so themselves? Yet Jesus "strapped the bomb" to Himself and died for the world. In a similar way, He calls us to follow His example. So, what will it be? As we kneel in the Garden of Gethsemane and cry out to God, whose will shall we choose?

Luke 12:15–34

Jesus tells his disciples a brief story about a man who, flush with the success of a good harvest, decides to build himself some big barns and retire early. May as well take it easy! First, notice verse 15: "Take heed and beware of covetousness; for one's life does not consist in the abundance of the things he possesses." Now clearly, there is room for having wealth and following Jesus, but great danger lies in abundance of possessions. They seem to have a way of possessing us, when we're supposed to see ourselves as their stewards—caretakers of God's things. This is what happened with the rich man; he made life all about himself. Notice the first- person pronouns all throughout verses 17–19. They appear at least 14 times in the New King James Version. That is why Jesus calls him a fool in verse 20 and then adds, "so is he who lays up treasure for himself, and is not rich toward God" (Luke 12:21).

This man is the poster child of many believers in America. They are so busy laying up for themselves that they do not even see how the world has grabbed their hearts. Let's do a little test. In many surveys the average believer gives roughly 3% of his income and wealth to the work of the Lord. That would mean he keeps 97% for himself. Clearly, the man is focused on his treasure, not Kingdom treasure.

Third, the Lord then adds in the remaining verses some amazing assurances:

1. Verse 22—Don't make life about your needs and wants.
2. Verse 23—Life is more than these things.
3. Verse 24–29—Let God take care of you and you focus on His call on your life.
4. Verse 30—God knows what you have need of before you ask.
5. Verse 31—Seek God and His call and let God provide for you.
6. Verse 33—Lay up treasure in Heaven, not on the earth.
7. Verse 33—Where your treasure is, there will your heart be (the reason for all of the above).

As Jesus closes this incredible passage with verse 34, He is greatly concerned with what has our hearts. He knows the power of the world and was tempted with it during His ministry as outlined for us in Matthew 4. He knows the power of the world, the flesh, and the devil, though ultimately, they did not affect Him. That is why there is so much emphasis in His teachings on just what, or Who, has our hearts. We are to pay the cost, but it will be more than worth the price.

John 15:19–20

Here, Jesus makes it clear we are not of this world. Case closed. For emphasis, He says it three times in verse 19: "If you were of this world," "You are not of this world," and "I have chosen you out of this world" (John 15:19).

There is no question—Jesus said we are not of this world. He wants us in the world but not of it. John makes this even clearer in John 17:14–18. Therefore, we have God's call to not be of this world but also not to hide from it. Unfortunately, the pull of the world is strong. Take a moment to contemplate how you are in the world but not of the world. If you give everything to Him, He can make it possible. You are going to lose your life either way. Why not do it according to His plan and will?

John 21

To get the best understanding of this last section, it would be worthwhile to pause and read John 21 entirely. It's quite a powerful passage! Let's summarize it before we get to verse 15. Jesus had died a few days earlier, and the disciples were rather discomfited. In John 21:3, Peter tells the others, "I am going fishing." Now, remember that he had left that years ago. There is no record of him ever returning after he walked out of the boat in Matthew 4. He had truly left it behind. But now, Jesus was dead, and Peter had no idea what to do. The nets have a way of drawing us back when we are in a time of confusion.

Jesus appeared to the disciples while they were fishing. They had toiled all night with no success, but He told them to cast their nets on the other side of the boat, which they did. They caught so many fish that they couldn't draw the net! Peter said that it must be the Lord, so he jumped out of the boat (not the first time he did that) and swam to the shore. Jesus provided fish and bread, and they ate together. Then, Jesus looked at Peter and asked him three questions. Or more specifically, He asked Peter the same question three times.

He asked Peter if he loved Him. Don't you find that interesting? Of all the questions to bring to Peter's attention, it is this one. Why? Because it sums up all that Jesus has been teaching. Those who love Him with all their heart, soul, mind, and strength truly have nothing left for the world to attach to. It is the same as the first commandment, which says we should have no other gods. Jesus is clear. It's Him and Him only. He wants our lives totally for Himself.

Now, when Jesus asked Peter this, He used the strongest word for love in the New Testament—*agape*. Peter responded with "You know I love you Lord," but he used the softer word for love—*phileo* (John 21:15). Jesus asked the same question a second time in the same manner, and Peter also responded the same way. Then, the third time Jesus asked, He switched to the softer word for love, and that grieved Peter's heart. Jesus had finally used the word Peter chose, and Peter *still* struggled to respond to that weaker word for love. Let's be honest—his behavior had not given Jesus nor himself any assurance that he truly loved the Lord, and Peter knew it. He had denied the Lord and returned to fishing after he had left it all behind. God would not even let him catch fish on his own. For Peter, there was no turning back.

This draws our attention to the very first question. In John 21:15, Jesus asks Peter the question "Simon son of Jonas, do you love Me more than these?" Here is where this whole passage becomes extremely interesting. What is Jesus referring to? Does "these" refer to the fish, boats, nets, disciples, or something else? Or maybe all of the above? Jesus does not say, and we can only assume what He may have meant or where He may have even been pointing. I am not sure it even matters totally, but the "nets" seem to intrigue me. The reason for this is the nets are what Matthew 4 says he left to follow. Of all the things, Peter left his nets. Included in that was also the boat, the fish, the family business, etc. Yet the text says "nets." Maybe this was his love? Maybe he often had days he wished he could have his hands in the nets, pulling them up, mending them, and catching fish.

The point for us is not whether Peter loves Jesus more than these, but do we? What would "these" things be for us? Our lives, our family, our career, our boats, our houses, our cars, our money, our fame, our wants, etc. Jesus does not play second to any other love. It is going to cost us to follow. We either pay now or pay later. Our choice.

TAKING THE CHAPTER A BIT FURTHER

1. Look over Appendix 1 and examine some of the different ones not included in this chapter. How do these challenge you about leaving all and following Him? Give some specific examples of what our Lord is telling you to do.
2. Summarize the heart of Jesus' teachings on the cost of following Him? Can you see any changes that need to be made in your personal life to put more focus on Jesus?
3. Do you think the apostles and early church understood the cost somewhat? How does their example in living this life relate to us?

Chapter 9

Jesus' Seven Powerful Statements About Losing One's Life

THERE IS NO QUESTION that Jesus made some very strong and demanding statements. God's Word and principles are timeless. They do not evolve, nor are they interpreted by changing culture. The timeless principles He gave while on this earth are just as valid today as when He gave them. His work is immutable just as He is immutable. So, what do we do with some of His strongest statements that are difficult to grasp?

In this chapter, I want to look at some of His strongest statements. Although these are mentioned in other places in the book, I have compiled them here for a more compelling impact. Over the next few paragraphs, we will examine these seven strong statements. It is important to note at the start that these passages are reasonably clear without any "deep" interpretation required. But they are difficult; we may not want to hear these truths or live them. The cost is not something to take lightly.

> *Statement #1: "He who loves father or mother more than Me is not worthy of Me." (Matt 10:37)*

Luke 14:26 adds a much stronger emphasis on this thought. Jesus says, "If any man comes to Me, and hates not his father, and mother, and wife, and children and brethren, and sisters, yea, and his own life, he cannot be my disciple." When combined, these two passages give very high standards for those who will choose to follow Christ.

There are several things to note at the beginning. One is that both of the strongest of emotions are included: love and hate. It would seem that there would be several options other than these two extremes. What about "Make Christ first and others second"? Or "Love Christ at least as much as you love your family"? These would certainly be more reasonable and palatable. Yet, the Bible consistently uses the two extremes to point out the battle of control over the heart. Matthew 6:24 states, "No man can serve two masters; for either you will hate the one, and love the other." The point in these and similar other passages is the same. You cannot love someone, give them your highest emotion, and then put anything next to them. There are no second places here. God is to be supreme and the only love of our hearts. When He is fully in that position, then it is possible to fulfill the other love responsibilities. They all flow out of the one true love that we ought to have. When you compare those loves, our love for God so far surpasses them that there are no "loves" left that will even come close. As a matter of fact, the others by comparison will appear more like "hate" than "love."

The danger of putting a love of any kind near our love for God is that it wants to take over the top spot. Being number two has only one passion: become number one. God wants all other loves in our lives to be so below our love for Him that some could construe it as hate. The word "hate" in Luke 14 is the word *miseo*, which is found 41 times in the New Testament. The word means "to hate or despise." Luke uses it later in the story that Jesus tells about Himself in chapter 19 regarding the parable of the ten pounds. There is little doubt that the one who is hated in verse 14 is none other than Jesus, who is hated by the Jews. That is part of the reason why they crucified Him. The word means hate, and Jesus telling us to hate has to be understood in light of His expectations for His followers.

There is no way to do this other than losing our lives. We have to come to the place where we accept that He is supreme and our sole love. Therefore, we forfeit anyone or anything that gets in the way of that love. Unless we live like this, we cannot be His disciples, and we are not worthy of Him.

> *Statement #2: "He who does not take his cross, and follow after Me, is not worthy of Me." (Matt 10:38)*

This is the second time in this passage that Jesus has asserted that some who claim to be followers and do not behave a certain way are not worthy of Him. *Worthy* is the same word used by the prodigal son, who no longer considered himself worthy to be called a son. Therefore, he was willing to come home and work as a hired hand in lieu of his new condition. Of course, the father would have none of that, but the word was fitting for how the prodigal felt about himself. He was no longer worthy. Jesus takes that same thought and applies it to the one who desires to follow Him but does not want to pay the cost. That person is not worthy.

Now, this leads us back to the beginning of this verse when Jesus explains that we must take up our cross. We need to be sure to clarify what that *cannot* means. He cannot be referring to a sore back, troubled marriage, cancer or some other discomfort that all of mankind might experience. It has to be something other than what a nonbeliever can experience. Otherwise, everyone would be carrying crosses as Jesus did, and that's highly unlikely. So, what is it?

There have been many studies about the meaning of this phrase. We don't want to complicate the point more than Jesus intended. As noted in earlier chapters, if the plain sense makes sense, seek no other sense. Well, plainly, Jesus isn't talking about going around carrying a wooden cross on our backs every day. But if you went back in time to Jesus' day and saw a man carrying a cross with soldiers all around him, you would know that man was a dead man. Jesus taught about "dead men walking" long before the phrase was popular. The idea takes us back to earlier truths of "living sacrifice," "dead to Christ," and "crucified with Christ." These are all consistent themes that originated from the words of Christ. "Taking up your cross" is synonymous with being dead to self and alive to God. In other words, the life I now have is because of Christ, and I live in Christ.

So what is Jesus' point? We are to lose our lives. We are to let go of our wants, wishes, and pleasures. We are to see ourselves as dead to self, this world, and anything that could take us from our intimacy with Jesus. That kind of living is costly.

Statement #3: "He who finds his life will lose it; and he who loses his life for My sake will find it." (Matt 10:39)

This section contains some of Jesus' clearest words to His followers about losing their lives. If this passage is truly all part of the same context of the full chapter, then it was given as He was sending out the disciples. He includes statements about death, being delivered up to death, falling to the ground, and losing one's life. Honestly, it would be difficult to read this passage and interpret it in light of present-day American faith. In fact, the statement appears at least seven times in the Gospels. Several are parallel passages, but the point that they are included in every Gospel is important:

1. Matthew 10:34–39—Lose your life
2. Matthew 16:24–26—Lose his life
3. Mark 8:34–38—Lose his life

4. Luke 9:23–26—Lose his life
5. Luke 14:25–33—Hate his own life
6. Luke 17:33—Lose his life
7. John 12:25–26—Hate his life

A careful look at the above passages will make it rather obvious that we are to lose our lives. If we take them at face value, we should see how Jesus clearly defines it. If you want to follow Christ, you are going to have to lose your life, meaning you are going to have to die to self and put Him as the supreme One in your life. You can no longer seek your will. You can no longer live life as you wish. Do you live this way? Is it a picture of the American church overall?

The meaning of Matthew 10:39 is based on the meaning of the word *lose*. What does it mean to lose one's life? The word implies to kill or to destroy. It is a basic word for *lose* in the New Testament that is found about 92 times. It is the same word used by the angel when describing that there were those who wanted to destroy the baby Jesus (Matt 2:13). The apostles used this word to describe how they were about to die in the storm on the sea (Matt 8:25). It means to die. Now, when you apply that meaning to this passage in Matthew 10, the meaning is as follows: he who chooses to make life about himself ("find his life") will discover in the end that he will actually lose it (he will fall short of the glory of God). On the other hand, the one who chooses to die to himself ("lose his life") will find that he will gain his life and so much more. In other words, this man will truly live life as God intended to the fullest and will be greatly blessed in Heaven forever more.

All this once again comes back to the challenge of what this life is all about. Do we get out of the boat and leave the nets conveniently or periodically, or do we say goodbye to it all and follow? Followers today in affluent America want their boats, nets, or whatever, and they follow Christ out of convenience. They want Heaven and earth at the same time, but Jesus emphasized that we cannot serve two masters.

Statement #4: "If anyone desires to come after Me, let him deny himself." (Matt 16:24)

Matthew 16:24–26 closely follows the words of Jesus in chapter 10. He is stating time and again that following Him is costly. It is not some soft follow. It is not some easy Jesus or a self-pleasure adventure. This is going to cost you your all. He closes this passage with a startling question in Matthew 16:26, which asks, "For what is a man profited, if he shall gain the whole world, and lose his own soul?" Should that not be cause for us to pause and reflect? It is clear that Jesus expresses a deeper truth than simply about the breath we breathe. If we walked into an emergency room, told the staff we were dead, and they took our pulse and heard us breathe, they would probably believe we were in need of psychiatric help. They would be right. So, what is Jesus' teaching?

The word here for *deny* only occurs eleven times in the New Testament (Matt 16:24, 26:34, 35, 75, Mark 8:34, 14:30, 31, 72, Luke 12:9, 22:34, 61). Jesus uses the word nine of the eleven times. The other two references are from Peter, who was responding to Jesus' statement that he was going to deny Him. Additionally, the word is always seen in a serious light. Finally, whatever Jesus said that the apostles and Peter would do in reference to Him (i.e., denying Him), He actually wants us to do in reference to ourselves (i.e., denying self). How are these two connected?

When Jesus tells us that we are to deny ourselves, we need to keep in mind that this has been His theme from the beginning. When the disciples got out of the boat, they left it all behind. Most importantly, they left what they wanted behind. They left their will, agenda, and future. From that point on, it was no longer about the self but about Him. Since our will desires to continually surface, Jesus reminds us that a denial of self must be an ongoing event. He distinguishes this in the verb tenses in this verse. Jesus uses an aorist when referring to both "deny self" and "take up the cross." That would imply making a decision with ongoing consequences and is why He uses the present tense for "follow Me." It is impossible to follow in the present and future if self continues to get in the way. Therefore, the call is to deny self initially and continue to deny it daily. We need to see ourselves as dead to self and alive to God and see our lives hidden in Christ.

Luke expands on denying self by adding the adverb *daily:* "If any man will come after Me, let him deny himself, and take us his cross *daily*, and follow me" (Luke 14:23, emphasis mine). Denial of self is not a one-time event. Everyday, we battle the self life. My will. My plans. My wants. Coming to Christ involves a surrender of all of that. No longer my will, but Thine be done. How does your life demonstrate that truth?

Statement #5: "For what profit is it to a man. if he gains the whole world, and is himself destroyed or lost?" (Luke 9:25)

In this passage, Luke explains a similar concept to what we've been seeing, but with a slight twist. Obviously, no man is able to gain the whole world because it lies in the hands of the wicked one. However, man can have such an earthly ambition that he becomes consumed with the world. This is why 1 John explains that we are to "not love the world or the things that are in the world" (1 John 2:15–17). In fact, John continues even further by saying that if we love the world, the love of the Father is not in us. Do we need to ask whom we love? Jesus asked Peter that question, and he wrestled with it because his behavior seemed as if he loved the world more than he loved the Lord.

Paul further amplifies this theme in Philippians 3:8 when he says, "I also count all things loss for the excellency of the knowledge of Christ Jesus my Lord; for whom I have suffered the loss of all things . . ." That phrase "suffered the loss" is the same word in Luke 9:25 that means "to be cast away." Do you see the connection? Either way, there will be a cost. If we choose not to follow, there is a cost. If we choose to follow, there is a cost. The only question is this: Which cost are we willing to pay?

> Statement #6: "So likewise, whoever of you does not forsake all that he has cannot be My disciple." (Luke 14:33)

Luke gave many of the same statements from other passages, such as "hate" family (which we discussed earlier), "hate his own life," and carry the cross. These themes are clearly mentioned numerous times in the writings of Jesus. Yet, in this verse Luke adds a deeper dimension to it all. It is almost as if he is saying, "If it has not been clear to you before, let's make it super clear. You need to forsake *all*."

The word *forsake* here is only found six times in the New Testament, but it gets the point across. Four of the times, it is used to say farewell when someone was preparing to leave the company they were with (cf. Acts 18:18). Take a moment, though, to look at this passage in Luke 14:33, and then keep its message in your mind while you examine Luke 9:61: "I will follow thee; but let me first go bid them farewell, which are at home at my house." Although at first glance the man appears to be sincere, it is clear with this connection that he is not willing to bid "home" farewell to follow Jesus. When we follow Him, we get out of the boat and say farewell to all. It is no longer our will to fish for fish. It is now His will to fish for men in His Kingdom work. Does He have your heart in this way?

> *Statement #7: "Unless a grain of wheat falls into the ground and dies, it remains alone; but if it dies, it produces much grain." (John 12:24)*

This is Jesus' seventh different statement that encompasses the theme of forsaking all. Undoubtedly, He is determined to get this theme across to the listener. How sad it is to see how few truly grasp the magnitude of His call. Here, He makes it known that a death must occur in order to follow Him (this is seen in verse 26). Just as in Jesus' time, many today want to follow Jesus, but on their own terms. Imagine if Peter had said to Jesus, "Yes, I want to follow, but we have some big fish to handle right now, so we will check in with you tomorrow." How do you think that would have gone over with Jesus? Yet people want to conveniently follow Him when it is easy, convenient, comfortable, and family-friendly.

The word for *die* in this passage is the main one used in the New Testament. Death of the person who decides to follow Jesus is necessary. The Scriptures later use words like *dead* or *crucified*. They all are saying the same things. To further emphasize that point, John adds the words of earlier writers by saying, "He that loves his life shall lose it, and he that hates his life in this world shall keep it unto life eternal" (John 12:25). The connection is made to all the other passages on this theme. In Chapter 4, I mentioned the October 1949 words of Jim Elliott who lost his life in Ecuador serving the Lord: "he is no fool who gives what he cannot keep to gain what he cannot lose." One would suspect that he had been meditating on passages like these.

Our Lord's strong statements simply cannot be dismissed. They must be practiced as a lifestyle for a believer or ignored with the knowledge that we are completely changing both Jesus' message and His examples to us. If Jesus had only mentioned the concept briefly and not shown it in his life, maybe an argument for a softer Jesus, a noncommittal Jesus who didn't inconvenience us, could be made. Yet, it is clear that He continues to repeat this truth over and over again.

This one principle lies at the heart of the cost of following Jesus. Is this life about me, about Him, or a little of both? He is to be Savior, but we all have lives as well. We determine how we live, how we function in this world, and how we move about. He is only included when our two lives (His and ours) intersect. If there is no particular overlap, we do our own thing. If He is relevant, then we look His way. It is often more true to say that Jesus is simply in our lives instead of actually being our Life. We have learned to make life about self while wearing the mask of Jesus. How have we managed to reinvent Him but then reassure ourselves that we are living the Christian life? Do we know that the last person to realize they are deceived is the one being deceived?

One extra thought worth adding to this chapter revolves around other "extreme" and difficult commands Jesus taught. He truly did not call for a soft following. He lived and taught of a high cost. His disciples did as well. Just consider these verses along with the thoughts in this chapter:

1. If you want to be great, learn to serve (Matt 20:26).
2. If you want to be first, be last (Mark 9:35).
3. If you want to be rich, give it away (Matt 19:21).
4. If you want to live, die (Matt 16:24–26).

Following Jesus is costly unless you redefine the Jesus whom you follow, a Jesus that is different than the one in the Gospels. However, that is truly not an option we have. We either follow the Jesus of the Bible, or we follow someone or something else. To follow the Jesus of the Bible is costly and nonnegotiable.

TAKING THE CHAPTER A BIT FURTHER

1. Read and meditate over Luke 14:25–33. Answer these questions
    a. Why did He speak in such strong words to the multitudes?
    b. If you were a disciple listening to this teaching, what may have been your response?
    c. When He says "you cannot be My disciple," what does that mean?
2. Is it possible to be a different kind of disciple that does not pay that kind of price in following Jesus? Explain.
3. What do you believe the "all" in Luke 14:33 means?

Chapter 10

Why Is There a Cost?

DID YOU EVER WONDER why followers of Jesus have to bear the cross? There may be a number of reasons. In one way it could be because the One we follow also bore a cross. He suffered and died, and so we are called to suffer and die as well. Another reason can be that the enemy hates us so much because of Whom we follow. Maybe it is part of this fallen world we live in. Maybe it is all of the above and more. However, there may be another reason that brings us all the way back to the Garden of Eden. Let me explain.

MAN CREATED IN THE IMAGE OF GOD

In the Creation account found in Genesis 1, God explains to us that man was made in His image. Genesis 1:27 says, "So God created man in His own image, in the image of God He created him. . ." This phrase is found several times in Scripture, such as Genesis 1:26, 27 (appears twice), 9:6, and also in the New Testament. It is clear that God made us in His image, but what exactly does that mean?

Well, let's clarify what it does not mean. It cannot mean something physical. God is Spirit and subsequently does not have an actual visual image. He can choose to put on an image, but that is not a true reflection of who He really is. He has no "image" that is physical. The Son of God took on the form of man, but that again does not reflect who He is. He was so much more than a physical representation. Thus, we will need to dig deeper into the Scriptures to see that answer exactly. Interestingly enough, it is connected to the cost. How is it possible that paying a cost for following Jesus is part of His plan to make us more like Him? Let's find out together.

MAN'S MARRED IMAGE

Here's the trouble: as a race, our image-bearing capability is limited. This is because man presently looks nothing like man before the Fall. Yes, we still have all the outward similarities of hair, eyes, nose, etc. But these do not make up the image of the person. The true image is so much more. Who really are you? I can say I am tall and Caucasian with grey hair, blue eyes, and a goatee. But is that truly the image of a person? When you take a photograph of someone, do you really believe you have captured the true image of that person? Are we so shallow that we believe what we are on the outside is actually who we are? Remember that "man looks on the outward, but God looks on the heart" (I Sam. 16:7). Why does God look on the heart more than the outward? Because He knows the outward does not reflect the true person.

Yet when Adam and Eve sinned, life as they knew it was no longer the same. Sin, death, pain, sorrow, thorns, heartache, and so much more became part of their lives that had not existed since their creation. They went from paradise to a sin-impacted world. In addition, something happened to this creation who originally were image bearers of their Creator. They still had the image of God in the strictest sense of being. That is why man was told to never take another man's life (Gen. 9:6). However, as we will see in the New Testament, that image is not the same today as the one from pre-sin Garden of Eden.

When man sinned, he did not change the outward image. Man still looked the same outwardly before and after the Fall other than the fact that decay had now set in. There is no evidence that man changed outwardly in some way besides his behavior. The physical appearance stayed the same. It was the inward that was marred.

GENERAL INFORMATION ON THE IMAGE OF GOD IN THE NEW TESTAMENT

The word for *image* is found 23 times in the New Testament. It will be necessary for us to look at many of these to get a firmer understanding of what the Bible means when it says that man was made in the image of God.

Matthew 22:20, Mark 12:16, and Luke 20:24

These parallel passages all describe the same event. The Pharisees came to Jesus to test Him about giving tribute to Caesar. He asked them to show Him the tribute money, and when they did, He asked whose image was on the coin. Obviously, it was Caesar's. He then gave His classic line: "Give to Caesar what belongs to Caesar and give to God what belongs to God" (ESV). The importance of this passage for our study is the usage of the word *image*. No one would say that the image fully represented who Caesar was. It was simply a coin that when examined, showed a clearly recognizable image of the current emperor. The coin was not Caesar; it just reflected his image. In the same way we are not God, but we are to reflect His image. One of God's purposes in saving us is to make us like His Son, but not make us His Son. That is all part of being changed into His image. But because of sin, the image that we should be bearing is not clearly seen. Therefore, He is working on us to change us into that image.

Romans 1:23

In this passage Paul describes the downward trend of mankind who continues to rebel and walk away from the true God. The verse claims that as part of mankind's decline, people "changed the glory of the incorruptible God into an image made like corruptible man, and birds, and four-footed animals, and creeping things" (Rom 1:23). Again, no one would believe that this human-created image was truly the complete reflection of the one it represented. In this case it was an extremely poor replica, if we can use that word at all. God cannot be made in man's view of Him. He is far beyond our comprehension or imagination.

2 Corinthians 4:4

Paul says that Christ "is the image of God." Now, what does that mean? Jesus said earlier that if you have seen Him, you have seen the Father (John 14:9). What did He mean? Was He saying that by seeing the Son, you actually see the Father? It would be unlikely that Paul meant seeing Jesus outwardly was actually the same as seeing the Father. Rather, he meant that if you have truly known Jesus, you have known the Father, especially since He came to declare the Father (John 1:18). Being God, Christ was the exact, perfect representation of the Father because He was equal with the Father. They have different roles, but in their essence, They made it so that to see One was to see the Other. This image is more about who the Father and Son are, not who they appear to be. Colossians 1:15 uses that same wording by stating that Jesus is the "image of the invisible God." An invisible individual doesn't have physical appearance, but who He is does not change, whether or not anyone can see Him.

Revelation 13:14, 15, 14:9, 11, 15:2, 16:2, 19:20, and 20:4

The last book of the Bible has the most occurrences of this word. It appears a total of eight times, and each refers to a similar context. Now, keep in mind that Satan is a counterfeiter. He is not creative, so he cannot come up with a novel idea. In the end times, he will do all he can to deceive; he has always been a deceiver. His last tactic will be to cause an unholy trinity to surface. This unholy trinity will consist of three members who will attempt to emulate the Holy Trinity. It will be a vain attempt, but because he is so deceptive, he will succeed greatly. This unholy trinity consists of the beast, the antichrist, and the false prophet. These three are all described in the book of Revelation. His work in the last days will be to cause an image of the beast to rise up. This image will expect all to worship him, take his mark, and serve him. He will claim to be the representation of the beast. To know the image will be to know the beast. It is just another attempt of the enemy to deceive mankind as he attempts to mimic the true picture of Jesus as the exact image of the Father.

THE IMAGE OF GOD RESTORATION

In several places in the Epistles, Paul explains the idea of a restored image. You can find it in Romans 8:28–29, 1 Corinthians 15:49, 2 Corinthians 3:18, Colossians 3:10, and their surrounding contexts. These passages help us understand that what happened in the Garden of Eden, although greatly tragic, is not a permanent problem. The Last Adam, Jesus, will one day restore all that the first Adam caused. Paradise lost will be Paradise regained. The lion and lamb will lay down together. The earth will be restored. The Last Adam will fix all that was tarnished, but His largest project is not the earth, which will eventually be destroyed anyway. His most incredible work is the changing of mankind from the image of the earthly to the image of the Heavenly. Let's watch how this is explained in the New Testament.

Initially, the Creator made the first Adam in His image. That image was then tainted with sin, and now man does not completely reveal his Creator. Instead, we bear a closer likeness to the image of Satan. We are in his hands and in our depravity reflect his character and will. That is why the Son came to "seek and save that which is lost" (Luke 19:10). But salvation is only step one in that process. Conversion to Christ does not make us final copies of the Savior. The potential exists, but we all know that we are a work in progress. Therefore, we need to be changed into His image on a regular basis.

Romans 8:28–29

Paul's major emphasis here is to lay out God's strategy for creating us in the image of Christ. By the way, if we already were sanctified, the new creation would not be necessary. So, salvation does not complete us; it just starts the completion process. These verses give us several key points:

1. All things are part of this plan of God. That would include "all things."
2. God makes the goal of all things good.
3. He has predestined this to happen; in other words, it will happen.
4. Those that are His are on a path of salvation (the first step in conforming to His image) and sanctification (the process of conforming us to His image) to glorification (being one day completed in His image) are all part of the process designed by God.

That process He takes each of us through is unique to each one, but the goal remains the same for all. That is why John says in 1 John 3:2 that one day we shall be like Him. Now, keep in mind that we will never have the essence of God. But we will have the pre-fall Adam image that was without sin. He is changing us daily towards His intended purpose.

1 Corinthians 15:49

This whole passage is worth your time to study, but for now, verse 49 really illustrates the point: "And as have borne the image of the man of dust, we shall also bear the image of the Heavenly Man." When did we bear the image of the man of dust? Contextually, the passage mentions the first Adam. Yet, it is doubtful that Paul is simply referring to Adam about his image because in a sense, Adam had two images—the image of God before sin and the image of God after sin. Which one would it be? It makes more sense to see this as the image of God we bear with all humanity, the one that we are born with and that also came from the first Adam, though in a different state than originally created. In that same way, we believers also have two images. We are born with the image of man and a weakened image of God, and one day we will have that God-image fully restored.

But then, Paul continues with this amazing promise. We shall one day also bear the image of the Heavenly. Here is the process of being changed from the image of God of the first Adam—which happens to all of mankind at birth—to the full image of Christ that awaits us in the Last Adam. We shall one day be like Him. The cost to follow Jesus is part of that process, but what an amazing reward!

2 Corinthians 3:18

It is easy to see the desire God has to change us into His Image. This verse makes it clear: "But we all, with unveiled face beholding as in a mirror the glory of the Lord, are being transformed into the same image from glory to glory, just as by the Spirit of the Lord" (2 Cor. 3:18). What a verse. Here, Paul lays out our journey as we are in God's program of change. The word for transformation here is where *metamorphosis* comes from. It is only found four times in the New Testament—twice in the Gospels to describe Jesus on the Mount of Transfiguration where He is changed into another image. The other two times are in this verse and in Romans 12:2. Now, you can clearly see the connection between dying to self and the transformation process. As we present our bodies a "living sacrifice," meaning alive in Christ but dead to self, we are being changed. That is the cost of following. That is the cost of Christlikeness. We must decrease, but He must increase. It is our cost, and true change only comes about when we follow Jesus with a cost.

Colossians 3:10

Salvation is just the beginning of a glorious process of being conformed to the likeness of Christ. Notice the wording in this sentence: "And have put on the new man, who is renewed in knowledge after the image of Him who created him" (Col. 3:10). The tenses of this verse further solidify the point I am trying to drive home. Believers have put on the new man (salvation). This new man (the restoring of the image of God) is to be renewed (present tense and ongoing). The end goal is the image of Christ, the One who created us. Again, it brings us back to the original creative work. God very directly puts us on the path of being changed to the likeness of His Son, conformed to His image.

This process, theologically called sanctification, has three components. First, there is positional sanctification where we are presently sanctified (1

Cor. 1:30). Second, we experience progressive sanctification, and we are all presently in this process whereby God is changing us into His image (1 Pet. 1:14–16). Finally, we will reach the perfect sanctification (1 John 3:1ff) so that one day we shall be like Him. What a journey!

THE IMAGE BEARING WILL COST YOU

When change happens, a clear struggle unfolds as the new works to overcome the old. If you have ever seen a caterpillar work at leaving its cocoon, you have witnessed such a struggle, and this is actually called metamorphosis, the same word for *conformed* that we highlighted earlier. In a caterpillar, the change occurs one way, and it occurs the same way for every caterpillar. In humans, God doesn't appear to conform to limited tools or methodologies in the process of creating change. Each human is a unique blend of learning, experiences, motivations, thoughts, and feelings. The process will not look identical for each person, at least not from our perspective. God will use pain and suffering, new experiences (sometimes shared and sometimes unique), and all kinds of things that will help chip the rough edges off our attempts to be like Jesus. We all need the change, we all need to work, and we all need the metamorphosis. One day, whether it's by the rapture or death, we will be changed.

Yet when we consider all the things that God uses to change us, the one thing that only believers encounter is the cost that comes from following Jesus. We share with the unbeliever the common cold, flu, heart disease, bad marriages, and a host of other earthly pains. But only believers solely share the cost that comes from following Christ. That cost alone is more transformative than any other single factor. How are you paying the cost? How are you becoming more like Christ? The journey is worthwhile as you will come forth from it as gold.

Those who know something about precious metals are aware that the greater the amount of heat that one applies, the greater the number of impurities that rise to the surface. The refiner knows the impurities are removed when he can see his reflection most clearly in the metal. We are God's greatest creation. He loves it when we reflect His image. Maybe our prayer ought to be "Bring it on. Make us like your Son so you can be most glorified in our journey for Him."

TAKING THE CHAPTER A BIT FURTHER

1. List some of the costs that you know people have paid over the years for following Jesus.
2. Why do some people seem to bear a greater cost than others?
3. Why is there even a cost at all for following Jesus?

Chapter 11

The Jealousy of God Demands the Cost

Part of understanding the cost is connected to better understanding God. God takes His relationship with His children very seriously. He is not One who "two-times," neglects, or forgets when He is in a relationship. Isaiah 49:15 states this truth clearly: "Can a woman forget her nursing child, and not have compassion on the son of her womb? Surely they may forget, yet I will not forget you." When we enter into a relationship with God called salvation, the commitment He has for us is so strong that He has given us the Holy Spirit to ensure our safe arrival to the other side. We may struggle with our commitment to Him, but He does not in His commitment to us. That is the doctrine of the jealousy of God for His children.

All theology and biblical understanding begin with a quest to know God. Who God is will determine our thinking about everything else. For example, God is holy, and out of that, we are to be holy. We only know this is our call because God is the source of it. Another example is that since God is love, we are to love. We only know love because He first loved us. But the one trait about God often overlooked in most theological circles is jealousy, and Scripture calls Him a jealous God. I believe this truth lies at the heart of understanding just what He expects of us and how we are to live.

THE DEFINITION OF THE JEALOUSY OF GOD

First, we need to understand the meaning of this term. Noah Webster's dictionary (my personal favorite) says jealousy is "That passion of peculiar uneasiness which arises from the fear that a rival may rob us of the affection of one whom we love, or the suspicion that he has already done it." The idea is that we love someone, and when someone steals that love, we become jealous. This is often found within a negative context. He is a very jealous man. She is a very jealous woman. The idea almost hints at a level of selfishness. However, the jealousy of God is not a human jealousy at all.

Mike Taylor, pastor of The Vine Church Teesside in England, tells us that "God always draws his people's attention to *himself*—not to personal holiness or social justice or any of the other good things that follow from a good relationship with God, but to himself. When his people's attention wanders from him, he's quick to draw them back." Taylor goes on to explain that this idea defines the jealousy of God, not as some negative, selfish emotion.[1] This is a holy jealousy.

Here is where the jealousy of God is absolutely different from the jealousy of man. God does not feel jealous over us because He is lonely, hurting, spurned, etc. His jealousy is holy and righteous. He is not jealous of us because He lacks anything and needs us to supply it. He is jealous over us for our loss. God has created us for Himself. He created us so He could pour Himself into us. This is an eternal pouring, so that in the ages to come, He might shower upon us more of His grace and blessing (Eph. 2:7).

The word *jealous* and other, similar terms occur often enough in the Old Testament that you can get a fairly clean definition of it. *Jealous* appears 18 times, *jealousies* once, and *jealousy* 34 times. We will look at many of the above references in this chapter. But before we do, let's settle on a definition that is clear for our study. God's jealousy is *His righteous possession of His children and His rightful ownership over them*. Listen to how Erik Thoennes says it:

> God is righteous and loving when he demands exclusive faithfulness from his covenant people. Because God rightly loves his own glory, and graciously loves us, he demands that we worship and serve him above all. In human history, God is most glorified by the undivided devotion of his redeemed people, and his ultimate jealousy for his glory demands this devotion. If he does not care when we love idols more than him, then he would allow himself to be dishonored and let us settle for less than we are intended to have from life. God's jealous love demands the best of us and our relationships.[2]

1. Taylor. "The Jealousy of God." 16 January 2004.
2. Thoennes. *Godly Jealousy: A Theology of Intolerant Love*, 216.

I believe he nails it. This is why the Lord will not share His glory or children with anyone. He is a jealous God, so no one dares mess with His children, and no child of His better mess with any other god over Him.

From the beginning of time, we see how God made creation to be a giver. He made the stars, sun, and moon to give light. He also made the sea, the grass, the trees, and the animals to give us food. God created after His kind. All of His creation in such a way resembles its Creator. God's jealousy is not an action on our part that completes Him in any way. We do not fill any emptiness in God. His passion for His sole ownership of us is solely about our need and His ability to fill that need. That is at the crux of why He is a jealous God over us.

THE FIRST EXAMPLE OF THE JEALOUSY OF GOD IN THE OLD TESTAMENT

We first encounter the jealousy of God for His people in a clearly identifiable way in Exodus 20. In this chapter, God brings Moses up on Mt. Sinai to give Him the law. Although there are more than 10 actual laws (some estimate as many as 613 total), the prominent 10 commandments receive the most attention. These 10 commandments are specifically divided into two sections. The first four focus directly on man's relationship with God. There are to be no other gods before the one true God. Man is not to make any graven image nor take the Lord's name in vain, but he should keep the Sabbath holy. These all consist of the vertical components of the commandments in man's relationship with his God. The Bible lists them first as a clear lesson that God is our first priority, and we cannot be right with man unless we are first right with God. Then, look a little more closely at the last six and you'll see how the vertical commands translate into our behavior with other humans. You shall honor your parents and not kill, commit adultery, steal, lie, or covet. These commands were given to teach mankind to deal properly with one another, and as such, they are classified as the horizontal commands.

It is rather intriguing that when the lawyer came to Jesus to test Him about the greatest commandments, Jesus brought his attention right back to the original 10 commandments. He said in Matthew 22 that we are to first love God with all our heart, soul, and mind. Luke even adds the word *strength*. Jesus then followed that command with the second statement that we are to love our fellow man. On these two truths hang all the law and the teachings of the prophets. Every law in the Old Testament can be connected to these two truths: love God and love your fellow man. If we lived by these two commandments, we could live up to the expectations of the Law. Paul even said that if we truly loved, then we would fulfill the entire Law (Gal. 5:14).

But it is the truth found in Exodus 20:5 that commands our greatest attention. God says "you shall not bow down to them (gods); nor serve them. For I the Lord your God am a jealous God" (Exod. 20:5). This means that He has given us these laws because of His character, and they flow out of a description of God. Namely, He is a jealous God.

THE EXPLANATION OF THE JEALOUSY OF GOD

God describes Himself as jealous. Our most common understanding of jealousy is not a positive image. We may think of a jealous boyfriend who goes on a rampage of harm and destruction because someone talked to his girl. Or of a jealous employer who works behind the scenes to destroy a competitor because his business is declining. Or maybe a jealous employee who may speak evil of another coworker just so only he can get the promotion. Jealousy is often associated with rage, envy, and other things that instill images of sin and sinful behavior. How can God describe Himself in such a way?

Remember that God's jealousy over us is all about His love and care for us, as well as Him wanting the best for His children. There is nothing selfish in the heart of God. This is why He is so adamant that we do not have any other gods before Him. He is to be the sole proprietor and resident in our hearts. He is to be our God and our God alone.

This also explains why He is so "angry" when we go after other gods. He will not be second to any. Time after time we hear well-meaning preachers and teachers discuss the priority scheme of the believer. It typically goes something like this. God should be number one in our lives. Well, that's a good place to start because it is absolutely true. The problem is what often follows that statement. We want to then put something as number two, number three, and so forth. What is wrong with that? Any time you put something as number two, what does the number two desire? There has never been a number two that does not desire to be number one. Also, keep in mind that nowhere in Scripture does such a false priority scheme occur. With God, there is no second, third, or any other competitor. He is to be the sole ruler, authority, and priority of our lives. When you put a second or third next to Him, you are stating that it would not take much for Him to be replaced. Don't you find it interesting that Jesus said you are to hate your mother, father, brother, sister, wife, or even your life? What was He saying? Don't you dare make anyone second to God.

But again, why is this important to God to be the sole ruler of our hearts? Simply put, when He is where He needs to be, all the rest will fall into place. Placing God as the number one in our lives permits Him to be the one who regulates all other loves we have. We can only love others when we love Him with all our heart, soul, mind, and strength. He did not say we should give him *most* of our love. Did you ever wonder how you can love others when you love Him with your all? The answer lies in the way God takes ownership and rulership of our lives. As He reigns supreme, we then are blessed with horizontal love that flows out of the vertical love, and it is our only and supreme priority.

THE NAME JEALOUS

But God takes this truth even further than just a description. His *name* is also Jealous. I would imagine that if you gave many believers a blank sheet of paper and asked them to list the names of God, this name would not appear. You would hear names like Yahweh, Jehovah, Lord, God, Jesus, Wonderful, Counselor, Mighty God, Prince of Peace, and others that are scattered all through the Scriptures. How often do you think you would see the name Jealous listed? Even if you examined numerous systematic theology texts, it would be difficult to find this name listed in any of them. Regardless of our perception, God gives Himself this name.

After Israel received the Ten Commandments, they also obtained other instructions about how they were to function as God's people. God gave them the Law in Exodus 20, and they were clearly called to be His peculiar people, a people unto Him and Him alone. In Exodus 24:3 they agreed to the terms of the Law and accepted this unique calling position of being the people of God. After this, they were given instructions about the temple where He would reside with only them. He took residence with no other people.

While God delivered the Law to Moses, Israel turned to idolatry at the base of the mountain (Ex. 32). God dealt with this sin, and they left Sinai. In chapter 33, He mentions the importance of His presence, which is forever to be a special trademark of His people (v. 14). Exodus 34 explains the second set of laws given to God's people. Moses had broken the first set in anger over their idolatry, and now God gave the Law to them a second time.

Watch how this unfolds in chapter 34. In verse 10 He reminds His people what He is about to do with and for them, again suggesting His particular affinity with Israel. God says in verse 11 that He will exterminate the inhabitants of the land. In the following verse He explains why, saying, "lest they become a snare to you" (Exod. 34:12). His concern is that these inhabitants with their gods will turn the hearts of God's people away from Him. Remember that they are to have no other gods before Him. He follows this in verse 13 with the demand that they are to destroy all of the idols and gods in a drastic and complete way. After these verses, God then reveals for the first time in the Old Testament His new name. Remember that the Old Testament revelation continues book by book for us to understand God. We don't learn all about Him in either of the first two chapters of Genesis. The Bible is like a curtain that God continues to open so we can see more and more of Him revealed bit by bit. Although we have watched His heart act out this truth in Exodus 34, we now also see His name clearly called Jealous. He is no longer just the God who is Jealous, but He is the God whose name is Jealous.

Meaning of His Name Jealous

It is one thing to say He is a jealous God, and another to complement that by saying the name Jealous. Just having the characteristic is certainly enough, but God is emphatic that we not miss the importance of it. But why did He take this as a name for Himself? Why should we call Him Jealous, as well as declare Him a jealous God?

It is all connected to the theme of Exodus. God has an absolute plan of bringing glory to Himself through His people. We, His most rebellious creation, are His treasure. He loves us and is committed to our wellbeing. That does not mean life will be easy. It just means that when everything is all over, we will see His hand and the good in it. The major part of this is His intentional plan to change us from depraved and rebellious at birth to His prized possessions at glory. Paul even hinted at that when he told the Thessalonians that they were his joy and crown at the appearing of the Savior. If Paul saw that in the Thessalonians, think how much more Our Lord sees that joy in His bride.

So, He puts the ring on our finger at the marriage betrothal time called salvation, and then He proceeds to conform us daily into the perfect bride who will be revealed one day in glory. When we stand before Him as His bride, we will be complete in Him. The cost we pay to be His joy and crown is submission to the pruning and development that must occur to make fallen man like Christ. It is no quick task, and for most, this will be greatly difficult. He did not promise it would be easy. He just promised us that one day it would be true. Is the cost worth it? On this side, many may wonder, but on the other side, no one will.

TAKING THE CHAPTER A BIT FURTHER

1. Look up any other references to "jealous" or "jealousy" in the Old Testament and see if you can discern the importance of this attribute of God. Why is it in the Bible? What can we learn about it?
2. Can you cite any parallels that we have today that compare to the jealousy of God?
3. How can God be jealous and not sin?

Chapter 12

All the Marks of a Follower Include the Cost

WITHIN THE OVERALL PLAN of Christ conforming and changing us is His master plan of discipleship. What makes this plan so important in the overall scheme is that He is not just conforming us into His image. It is not simply a plan to individually change us for His glory. Yes, that will happen. But the path of changing us is also one in which He expects our involvement with others, to bring them along. Some like to call this process "disciple making." So, while He conforms us into His image, He also makes us into disciples. These disciples are then to be involved in making other disciples. You can see that process of development throughout His ministry on the earth. Then, when He prepared to depart, He explained to His disciples that they were to go out and do the same as He did. Disciples make disciples. As He changes us, He desires that we assist others as they change into His image.

When I was a child, my mom's parents lived two houses down the street from me. They were my only grandparents who were still alive. Dad's parents had died long before my birth. My grandmother could make the best fudge in all the world. Many Friday nights when we all gathered at her house, the stove would be active. The smell would draw us before the food was even ready. When my grandmother died, so did that fudge recipe. Sadness still wells up in my heart over the loss of that recipe. Much more alarming, however, are the many truths that God pours into His followers daily that are never passed on to others. God does not change us simply to reflect His glory. There is so much more to it. He is changing us so that we can help others change, as well. That, my friends, will cost us.

Just a brief note here: some of this material will correspond with Chapter 9, although here the emphasis will be different. In Chapter 9, I attempted to compile some of Jesus' hard statements in order to understand their connection to the cost of following. For this chapter, I hope to focus on discipleship. Although there is a distinct overlap, the direction of these two chapters is different.

WHAT IS A DISCIPLE?

Before we go into the marks of a disciple, let's first be sure we understand the word accurately. Two Greek verbs translate to *disciple* in the KJV—*manthano* and *mathateuo*. From these two Greek words, we find 29 occurrences of *disciple*. You may see these translated as *disciple*, *teach*, *learn*, or something similar. The idea behind it is that someone is under another person and learning what that person teaches him. He is being "discipled."

Discipleship is important because it is the exact plan our Savior put in place for developing the church. The church is a fellowship of many coming together for His glory and each other's edification. We are all to be part of the body that is called the church. We each have our own gifts, and the church functions more efficiently when we all do that to which we have been called. Disciple making is a major part of that calling. Matthew 28:19–20 says we must make disciples, not converts. It is the call of helping believers mature in their faith on their journey to Christlikeness.

Would you call yourself a disciple? Are you under someone's teaching and training to be all God has called you to? Additionally, are you a disciple maker? You cannot let what God pours into you die on the vine. It must be given out for their growth and His glory. At some point you have to realize that God is not just making you like Himself solely for you to mature. It is also for you to mature others.

To further see how this connects, we must remember what Acts 11:26 says: "The disciples were first called Christians in Antioch." So, when we use the words *disciple* or *Christian* today, we should be discussing the same person. On the day we follow, we become His disciple and a Christian simultaneously.

But what does a disciple look like? It is one thing to be part of a process, but it is another to know where we are going. Our Lord gave seven distinct characteristics for a disciple to have and for us to know what we are aiming for. These are clearly stated in the Gospels in passages that we have already examined. The marks have a different angle than the other chapters but fit nicely into the overall thought of this book. In all the years of ministry, nothing has been more draining than disciple making, and nothing is more rewarding. This is part of the cost. Are you willing to pay it? It is costly to be a disciple of Jesus, and it is also costly to be a disciple maker.

THE SEVEN MARKS OF A DISCIPLE

These seven marks that identify disciples of Christ are not to be used as a list of required elements for perfection. This is just a list given Jesus gives us to help us keep on track. As we disciple, our goal is Christlikeness for everyone whom we pour into.

> *Mark #1: A disciple is one who loves Christ supremely, or they cannot be His disciple. (Luke 14:26)*

This first mark is the best way to start this section. Whom do you love? It has always been the first and most important question that a disciple must answer. When Peter and the others left the boat, they had to wrestle with it. "Do I leave the boats, nets, and family behind, do I hold on to both, or do I love the Lord supremely above all?" Their answer was the same one Jesus gave the lawyer who wanted to know the most important commandment. Without hesitation, Jesus told him to love God with all his heart, soul, mind, and strength. This idea also ties into the first of the 10 commandments in Exodus 20 where He says, "You shall have no other gods before Me" (Exod. 20:3).

How would you measure whether you're putting God first in your life? Maybe it begins with a brief survey of the three most important things that you have: time, talents, and treasures. Look at the hours of the day. How much of your time is spent in prayer, Bible reading, meditation? How much of your time is dedicated to intentionally working for His purposes, no matter what activity you're engaged in? Is He just in your life, or is He your life? What about your talents? Do you use them for God or for self? Or what about your treasures? Does He own it all, and you are merely a steward? Remember that we reproduce after our kind, so if we are a weak disciple, we will reproduce weak disciples.

Let's meditate on this very important truth before we look at the others. The only question Jesus asked Peter after his denial was "Peter, do you love Me more than these?" (John 21:15). You can fill in what the "these" are. Start with your name. Do you, ___________, love Me (Jesus) more than

__________? Jesus then adds the important statement that if you don't love Him supremely, you cannot be His disciple.

If Christ is not your first love, then this is a clear mark you are not His disciple. Now, few may feel they qualify to be a disciple with such a strong expectation as this. (But don't forget the influence of the Holy Spirit in the process!) However, this is what Jesus said and exactly what He meant. Our goal every day is to love Him this way. That, my friends, will cost you.

Mark #2: A disciple is one who bears their cross, or they cannot be His disciple. (Luke 14:27)

In the very next verse to loving God supremely, Jesus adds the second mark, which reads, "And whoever does not bear his cross and come after Me, cannot be My disciple" (Luke 14:27). We have discussed what that means in an earlier chapter. There's no need to rehash it in depth, but let's at least remind ourselves of this truth. If we make life about us and not Him, then we are not disciples. Peter and the others did not say to Jesus that they would follow part time. They left the boat and died to their will, wants, and wishes. "No longer I, but Christ" was their mantra. No looking back. The cross was before them, the world behind, and they would not turn back.

Unfortunately, too many want to follow Jesus and be of the world. They want both. But Jesus is direct: following Him requires a death. You can follow, but it will cost you your life. This is what a living sacrifice is today. We are simply dead men walking with the life of Christ. He died; therefore, we died. He lives; therefore, we live, but only as He is the life living through us. Without Him, we have no life. That will cost us.

Jesus again closes this mark with His strong statement about discipleship. If you don't bear your cross (i.e., be a living sacrifice), then you cannot be His disciple. How much more clearly does Jesus have to say something before we get it? This might explain why the church is so weak today in America. We have followers who have never died to themselves. Jesus says this cannot be. When was your funeral? If it did not happen on the day you gave Him your life, then maybe you need to revisit that commitment and surrender anew to Him and His sovereign rule over your life. It will cost you, but it will be so worth it. There is nothing about self that is worth keeping.

Mark #3: A disciple is one who counts the cost, or they cannot be His disciple. (Luke 14:28)

Right after Jesus states the first two marks, He gives a parable about counting the cost, and this is where we get the title for this book. Jesus makes the connection to discipleship with the first words: "for which of you." "Which of you" refers to the disciples. Which of you who claim to be disciples "sits not down first and counts the cost" (Luke 14:28, KJV). Now let's investigate this further. I doubt many people truly count the cost on the first day of surrender. Did Peter, John, James, and Andrew fully understand what getting out of the boat meant? Of course not. None of us do. So, what did Jesus mean? The idea is not that we fully understand all that the cost means, but that we have surrendered our own will so that we are willing to count the cost. We cannot follow unless we surrender that will.

This parallels the concept of Lordship salvation. It is probably impossible for someone to come to Christ fully understanding what His Lordship means, but it is also impossible to be saved unless one first believes with their heart that He is Lord, whether they understand it fully or not. If Peter had looked at Jesus and then at the nets and couldn't decide which to follow, then he wouldn't be a follower at all. He couldn't halfway follow Jesus. Jesus added this thought right in the middle of the cost of following Him: Don't make a hasty decision to follow. This journey is not a joy ride. It is not some "Get Out of Hell Free" card. You may not have understood that when you started the walk, but if you are not following Him with that cost-focused mindset, then you need to ask what or whom you are following. Jesus is costly to follow.

Mark #4: A disciple is one who forsakes all, or they cannot be His disciple. (Luke 14:33)

Luke writes the most extensive passage on the cost of following Jesus. I wonder if maybe he left the medical community to be a follower as well. There is no evidence either way, but if he did, he certainly would understand the cost. When he closes this lengthy section, he adds a phrase no one else included: "Whoever he be of you that forsakes not all that he has, he cannot be my disciple" (Luke 14:33, KJV). It is almost as if Jesus is saying to the disciples, "If you have not gotten the point so far, then let Me sum it up for you." He wants their all.

Absolute submission to the Lordship of Jesus is not an option. It is the life we have been called to live. Not I, but Christ. One of the best ways to see this picture is with this visual. Imagine a pie with 10 slices. You can write something on each slice as it describes your life. One slice is work, one is family, one is recreation, one is church, and one is Jesus.

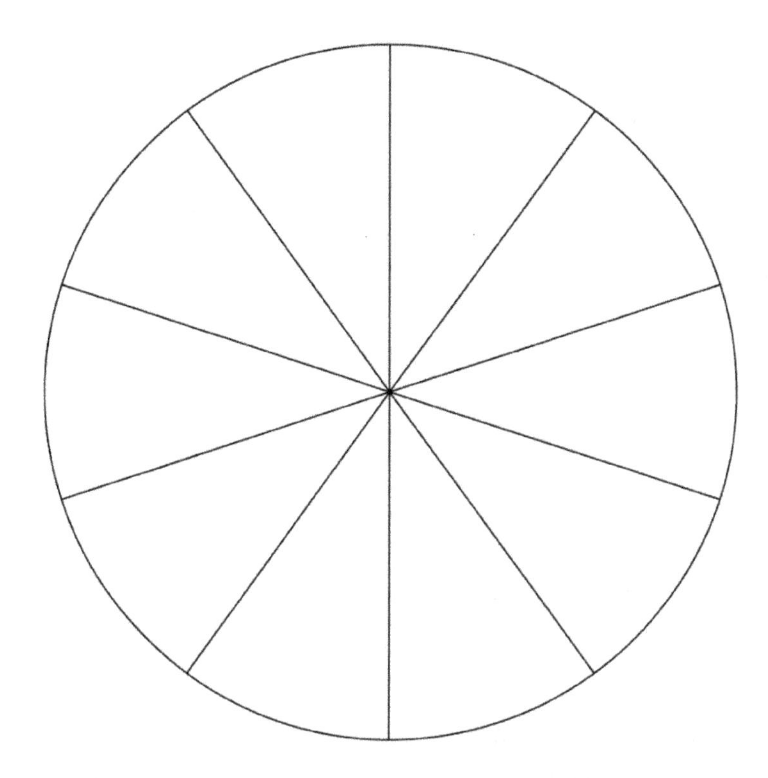

You can fill in the other slices with whatever fits. Does that picture describe your life? In that case, Jesus is just one part of your life. He is simply in your life. The problem with that is the picture is not accurate. Jesus has no interest in just being in your life. He desires to be your life. Colossians 3:4 says that Christ is our life. Period.

Now, picture the pie again. This time, cut out a middle circle of the pie first and put Christ's name on it. Out of that circle, all else exists. Yes, we have a job, family, etc. They are all part of our lives. But they only have meaning when they flow out of the centrality of Christ and Christ alone. With this visual you can see that Christ is your life, and He leads the rest of it too.

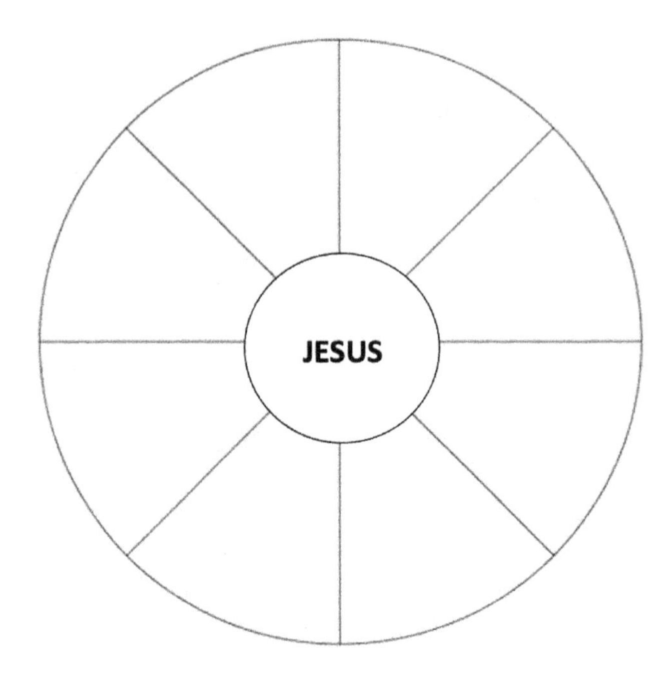

Jesus then adds for the third time the phrase found earlier in the first two marks: "If you do not forsake all, you cannot be My disciple" (Luke 14:33). He does not say you are close to being His disciple. He does not say you are somewhat His disciple. He does not say you get credit for trying. He is clear that you either are His disciple, or you are not. Which is it with you? And don't think for one moment it comes cheaply. There are too many people today living cheap grace. Grace is neither cheap nor easy. It is just free. So is Christ. But He is costly to follow. That is why many will say, "Lord, Lord did we not. . ." and He will respond, "I never knew you" (Matt 7:22–23). Unwillingness to pay the price is evidence of someone who is not a disciple.

> *Mark #5: A disciple is one who continues in the Word, so shall they be His disciple. (John 8:31)*

We now leave Luke to see that the final three marks are recorded for us by the Apostle John. In this fifth mark found in John 8:31, Jesus emphasizes the importance of the Word, saying, "If you continue in My word, then you are My disciples indeed." Although John words it slightly differently, it is the same thought. Here, instead of "you cannot be My disciple," he puts a more positive spin on it. It is important to note that Jesus connects the position of being a disciple with the value of the Scriptures. To phrase it another way, how can you say you are following Him when you have no desire to be in the Word? It just does not make sense. You cannot say that you are a disciple when the Word is not a priority.

Similarly, the apostle John explains, "He that abides in the doctrine of Christ, he has both the Father and the Son" (2 John 9). How can you say you are a follower when you have no desire to be in His presence? If Peter had said to Jesus, "Yes, I will follow you but have no plan to listen to you teach," do you think that would have been acceptable to Jesus? Here are some other Scriptures that might help answer that:

- Joshua 1:8—"This Book of the Law shall not depart from your mouth, but you shall meditate in it day and night."
- Psalm 1—The blessed man is the one who delights in the Word.
- 2 Timothy 2:15—We are to study to show ourselves approved unto God. (The word *approved* suggests being tested. Our delight in the Word is a sign of discipleship.)
- 1 John 2:3—"Now by this we know that we know Him, if we keep His commandments." (We cannot keep His Word and not be in His Word.)
- 1 John 2:5—This verse even says it is proof that we know Him. Then, is it not proof that we do not know Him if we neglect His Word?
- 1 John 3:24—"He who keeps His commandments abides in Him."

Now, does 2 John 9 teach that if someone claims to be a follower but is not in the Word, then that person is not follower at all? That is extremely tough to measure, but it seems like this verse is suggesting rather emphatically that you are giving more evidence of not being a follower than being one. That alone should cause one to seriously look at their time alone with God. The commitment will cost you, but it will surely be worth it.

Mark #6: A disciple is one who loves one another, and therefore, so shall they be His disciple. (John 13:35)

It seems extremely fitting that a mark of a true follower includes the importance of loving one another. The verse before makes it even stronger because Jesus says, "A new commandment I give to you, that you love one another; as I have loved you, that you also love one another" (John 13:34). This action is also non-negotiable for the follower of Jesus. He is the Master Lover of our soul and is known for His love. The most well-known verse in the Bible is about His love for the world (John 3:16). There are many verses that support just how much He loves us, even while we were sinners and even when we do not live as we should. However, love is a definitive characteristic of Christ and should be of His followers. By the way, truly loving others will cost you.

John adds more clarity to this truth in his first epistle. Check out these verses:

- 1 John 2:10—"He who loves his brother abides in the light . . ."
- 1 John 3:14—"We know that we have passed from death to life because we love the brethren."
- 1 John 3:17—"But whoever has this world's goods, and sees his brother in need, and shuts up his heart from him, how does the love of God abide in Him?"
- 1 John 4:7—". . . everyone who loves is born of God and knows God."
- 1 John 4:8—"He who does not love does not know God . . ."
- 1 John 4:12—"If we love one another, God dwells in us . . ."
- 1 John 4:16—". . . he who abides in love abides in God . . ."
- 1 John 4:21—". . . he who loves God must love his brother also."

John, often called the apostle of love and the apostle whom Jesus loved (as seen in John 11:3), also wrote the most on this subject. In John's eyes, under the inspiration of the Holy Spirit, how dare anyone say they love God, whom they have not seen, but do not love their brothers, whom they do see? When the God of love pours His life into us and develops that love in us as we journey, we can reasonably expect that love to flow out of us. Loving like this is natural for the follower, but no one said it was easy. Paul even said that "as much as lies in you, live peaceably with all" (Rom. 12:18), which implies that not all of the family will be easy to love. Sometimes, we may need to confront and chastise. Yet we will never have a reason not to love one another. This kind of love will cost you. It is the love that Jesus is and lived, and He expects us to emulate it.

He closes this one the same way as in John 13: "If you love, so shall you be My disciple." It is the positive spin on the negative that Luke used. This kind of one another love turned the world upside down during the early church period. It was even said of them, "Behold how they love one another." The origin of this phrase is uncertain but has been attributed to Aristides the Athenian. Would that be said of the church today? In order for that to be true, believers would have to pay the cost of dying to self and living as Christ has called us all to do.

Mark #7: A disciple is one who bears fruit, so shall they be His disciple. (John 15:8)

The final mark mentioned in the Gospels by Jesus is found in John 15:8. It is the mark that occurs while He discusses the value of being in the Vine, which is really a reference to Himself. In John 15:1 He calls Himself the True Vine and then says that if a branch (i.e., professed followers) does not bear fruit, He takes them away. Every branch that bears fruit He purges so that it may bear more fruit. He explains in verse 4 how it is necessary to abide in the Vine in order to bear fruit. He adds again in verse 6 that if a man abides not in Him, He will cast them forth into the fire. His point is that non-fruit-bearing, professing followers are not possible. These are the points He gives:

1. Followers abide in the Vine.
2. Abiding in the Vine means fruit will grow, and we see that in trees today.
3. If no fruit is yielded, then the branch is not abiding.
4. It is impossible to abide and not bear fruit.

Then He gives His final thoughts on fruit bearing in verse 8: "Herein is My Father glorified, that you bear much fruit, so shall you be My disciples" (John 15:8). As before, John gives a positive take on the mark by stating that our abiding is proof we are His disciples. God takes it personally upon Himself to prune His followers while they are on this journey to become like Christ. Pruning is part of the cost. He may have to prune our attitude. He may have to prune our tongue. He may have to prune our thought life. To have no pruning at all would be a strong statement that you are not one of His followers and are not in the Vine.

The one thing that is missing in this final mark is a description of what the fruit may be. If we apply the analogy of the fruit, the vine, and the branches to what is known from nature, it would appear to be something like this: if you are an apple tree, you produce apples. If you are a pear tree, you produce pears. If you are a disciple, you produce disciples. This is the call given to us in Matthew 28.

Being a follower of Jesus is costly. Your salvation costs you nothing. It is a free gift from God. However, the gift will change you and make you into the man or woman God wants you to be. Your salvation came with no cost, but to follow Him will cost you everything. May we all lose our lives now for the Kingdom call.

TAKING THE CHAPTER A BIT FURTHER

1. For further study, you can examine the idea of the cross in the six passages it occurs (Matt 10:38, 16:24, Mark 8:34, 10:21, Luke 9:23, and 14:27). Jesus tells us in the Gospels six specific times that we are to take up our cross. Yes, these are also parallel passages, but the New Testament includes them several distinct times. Compare and contrast these instances and develop a picture of what "taking up our cross" means.
2. List some marks today that should follow a believer in Jesus. What could be concluded about a professing follower if there are no marks?

Chapter 13

A Reinvented Jesus Dismisses the Cost

All the statistics that come out about the church in America are dismal at best. We hear things like the divorce rate is no different between followers of Jesus and those who do not follow. Christian men struggle with pornography as the world does. Christians overindulge in alcohol on a level similar to the world. The language of the believer and nonbeliever is similar. We could go on and on with statistic after statistic. The one thing that seems to continually surface is that the Jesus of the New Testament and the Jesus lived out in many American lives today appear to be two different people. One of two things has to be true. Either the Jesus of the New Testament cannot be taken literally for our time, or we have reinvented Jesus to fit our comfort zone. Let me offer a few pictures that have surfaced today of the Jesus we presently promote in some circles of faith. Some of these certainly will seem to overlap, but they have been added to make sure the picture is as clear as possible.

SOME EXAMPLES OF A REINVENTED JESUS

Liberal Jesus

This is the Jesus that not only loves everybody but also accepts everybody regardless of their beliefs or their sin. The emphasis here is on "accepts." There is no question that Jesus loves everybody. John 3:16 makes that clear. The problem lies in the acceptance of all regardless of sin.

To make Jesus some kind of soft, loving, person with whom everyone is accepted and free to live any way they want is an affront to His holiness. Yes, He welcomes anyone to come to Him but He in no way accepts their sin and does not permit them to continue in that sin. The woman caught in adultery in John 8 is a classic example of this. Did He unconditionally receive this woman? Absolutely. Did He unconditionally accept her lifestyle? Absolutely not. She was living an adulterous lifestyle that was not permissible for one who belongs to Him. Therefore, He told her in John 8:11, "Neither do I condemn you. Go and sin no more."

His statement of no condemnation was not an approval of her past. It was a statement about both her present situation and her actions going forward. He has no desire to condemn anyone, but if they choose a lifestyle that is forbidden in Scripture, then they bring the condemnation upon themselves. Our unrepentant sin condemns us. Jesus does not have to.

The liberal Jesus is one that receives all. But then we can live contrary to the Scriptures and still be in favor with God. This is a reinvented Jesus that does not line up with the New Testament. This Jesus has been reinvented in many denominations until he doesn't even look like the Jesus the Bible presents at all.

Wrathful Jesus

This particular Jesus was invented as something of a reaction to that soft, accepting, doormat sort of Jesus. This wrathful Jesus is one that is waiting to zap you as soon as you step out of line. He has rules and regulations which are only invented to make your life miserable. He is known more for what He is against than what He is for. Extremely fundamental churches can drift into this mentality. All you hear from them is what God hates and how that wrath and judgment are coming.

Yes, judgment and wrath will occur, but that does not take away from the grace and love of God. He is so gracious that He is willing to permit the likes of us into His Heaven simply if we apply faith to His name. By believing, sinners are redeemed for His glory. Wrath abides on the unbeliever, but the believer is no longer under the wrath. All that He does in the believer's life is designed to bring that child into His likeness. He disciplines and may even rebuke us, but the wrath of God has been appeased by the work of Christ on the cross. The unbeliever abides under God's wrath but is only a prayer away from grace. The more we can present Him as a God of grace, the more He can be seen as the true God that He is. Should they resist Him, they will meet Him in His wrath. If you are not a follower, please accept Him now as the gracious God that He is so that you will never see His wrath.

Indifferent Jesus

This claims that there is a God in Heaven, but He is either very preoccupied or just indifferent. We live our lives as we wish because we are the gods of our own lives. We make our decisions and live accordingly while He sits in Heaven, unconcerned and detached from our lives. He simply does not care. According to this idea, we know He doesn't care because if He did, He would never let evil run as wild as it does. If He really cared, life would be less complicated and evil. God does exist but could not care less about this life.

Again, this is such a gross misunderstanding of the true Jesus. He came and gave His life to redeem mankind from the horrible trappings of sin and the coming judgement for sin. By making Him indifferent, we have made the cross ineffective and His life and teachings useless. In this mindset, this kind of Jesus is useless to our lives, and we just need to make the best of this life on our own. It is all up to us. This kind of Jesus can be discovered more in the company of deists. Jesus may not even exist at all to them, and life's really not spiritual at all.

The "Whatever You Want to Make Him" Jesus

In this view, Jesus is whatever you can make Him out to be. He can be loving, wrathful, indifferent, detached, friendly, or whatever. It can even change from day to day. He is what we want to make Him out to be. We look at life through our lens, and God simply spins on the point on which we put Him. Relativism is close to this kind of thinking. Life is more about us and whatever religion can do for a person on that particular day.

The Out-of-Context Jesus

We see this often when passages are quoted out of context. A classic example is Matthew 7:7, "Judge not, that you be not judged." If you are ever in a conversation with someone about what is right or wrong today, this verse may just get slammed in your face. The person probably has no relationship with Jesus but knows enough about the Bible to be dangerous. "Judge not" becomes the mantra for the out-of-context Jesus followers.

They also use the fact that Jesus ate with sinners as an excuse to live recklessly close to the line. Yes, Jesus did eat with sinners, but Jesus was also sinless. If we could reach the place where we were sinless, we would have a better chance of eating with pagans without being tainted. That is not to say that there are not times we are to be with those without Christ. They need to see Jesus in us, and we need to engage the world. Christians with an out-of-context Jesus, however, use this verse as an excuse to live as the world does.

The only way to study Jesus properly is to handle the Word accurately. Once we become our own interpreters of Him and His teachings, we risk misquoting Him and taking His words out of context. Know the Bible before you talk about Jesus.

The Hippie Jesus

It is doubtful that few reading this section will even remember the hippie movement. During that time period, Jesus became a "fad," and was actually quite popular. Even some of the rock musicians, such as the Beatles, talked about Jesus in their songs. In the late 1960s, some churches even welcomed hippies into their family, such as Calvary Chapel in Costa Mesa, California. This was revolutionary because, at that time, people were often prohibited from even entering churches if they didn't have the right hair and clothing styles. The movement's ideas of peace and love looked more like a "real" Jesus than what some churches were presenting. Hence, this movement became very popular among the youth.

Since many of the pictures have Jesus with long hair, Jesus fit right in with this hippie crowd. Was it permissible to have long hair, smoke pot, live off the land, dress scantily (or not at all), and embrace the other similar characteristics of this movement and still be a follower of Jesus? That question often provoked much discussion in those trying to be the world and not of the world.

When you look today at the culture around the church, you may find some of that mindset still in place. We need to be careful to have a proper balance between the world and the church. Far too often the world has more influence on the church than the church has over the world.

To sit and battle these issues individually can be a project of futility. Does Jesus care what I wear at church? Does Jesus care if I have a hat on or wear jeans with holes? Does Jesus care if we sing songs that are contemporary and sound like rock music? Does Jesus care if I have tattoos, piercings (more present-day concerns), or whatever else that we may deem important to our liking? Again, to debate all of this could be futile. My suggestion is always to be aware of the culture and the traps contained therein. Far too much attention is focused on the issues that overall have little eternal value. The hippie movement may have thrown many of those concerns to the wind, but they still become cause for dissension in the church. Yet whatever the passion was during the hippie movement that motivated them to search for the true Jesus, that passion is something we still need today.

The Weak and Timid Jesus

The Jesus of this view differs little from the liberal Jesus mentioned earlier. The big distinction is that this Jesus is really the Jesus of the Bible, but it focuses solely on only a couple of His characteristics: His softness and peace. The view sees Jesus as a soothing song or a calming ocean. He speaks softly and carries no stick at all. What the world needs, proponents say, is sweet love, and Jesus is just the one to help us think happy thoughts. Let's just be like Him in this world and make it much a better place. Conflict should be avoided at all costs, because this Jesus wants us all to be friends.

I doubt that these people have ever read the passages where He overturned the tables or where He called Peter Satan. And I doubt that they have ever studied the cross and how horrific it was. He was neither weak nor timid. He was more of a "man's man," the carpenter-type, and He was not afraid to take on the religious elite of the day. This Man was fearless, and He was not at all concerned about conflict. He was zealous for the truth, even when His disciples or His family thought it was too offensive. Jesus is anything but weak and timid.

Prosperity Jesus

As you engage Christian culture today, you will find a gospel that preaches a Jesus who is the ultimate wish-granter. Some of the prosperous spokespeople for this Jesus have their own jets, lavish houses, large bank accounts, and fame status. They preach that this Jesus really does want everyone to be happy, to find personal fulfillment, to have all there is to have. All we have to do is pray the right prayer, donate the right amount of money, believe hard enough, and it will all be ours—Jesus is just waiting to give.

The Jesus of the Bible had no place to lay His head. He had no donkey of his own to ride on and instead needed to borrow one. He had no room for the last supper and borrowed that, as well. He had no grave of His own when He died but was buried in a borrowed tomb. Jesus died with nothing at the end of His life other than the clothes on His back, which were gambled for at the cross. And as we have seen, He preached cost, not easy living. He spoke of the dangers and deceitfulness of riches.

Yet somehow this prosperity Jesus continues to be famous all over the world. How can those who promote a prosperity Jesus reconcile the two widely differing pictures? It is all part of the reinventing of Jesus. If we can portray Him differently long enough, people will buy into it. We need to get back to the Jesus found in the Bible and stop making Him fit into our mold.

My BFF Jesus

With social media acronyms ruling much of our lives now, it stands to reason that we should have a BFF Jesus. BFF stands for *best friend forever*. We also hear Him talked about as our pal, co-pilot, and drinking buddy. He is lowered to the level of any friend that we may have. We just hang out together.

While it is good to have Jesus close to us and to walk this journey with, we must never forget who He is. He is King of Kings and Lord of Lords. This view, though it sounds pleasant, ignores His holiness completely. Jesus did eat and hang out with his disciples. He laughed and talked with them. But He showed them quite clearly that He was *not* like they were. He was holy and righteous, and He was there to create change, not to catch up on the latest sports scores.

He is *not* our BFF, and He should not be messed with. If God walks with us, it is to shape us into the image of His Son. He is looking to change us, not just hang out with us. He is looking to chip away the coldness of our hearts and set them on fire with His passion. He is not looking for a companion. He is looking for a vessel to mold for His glory and purposes. It is ok to hang out with Jesus, but we need to be sure we know who He is.

The Advisory Jesus

It is often easy to think that Jesus caters to our needs like calling a helpline to fix our computers. We dial Him up and ask Him what to do, and once He tells us, we go on our merry way. He is an advisor to us but only when we need Him. If life is good, then we set Jesus aside in the closet for another day. If a crisis occurs, we call on Him. He will advise us what to do. Sadly, with this Jesus we miss out on the wonderful life that He offers us through all circumstances.

The Redefined Jesus

The above examples, although certainly not exhaustive, are just a sampling of the way we reinvent Him. We read into the text what we believe it says rather than let the text tell us what it means. We seek a no cost Jesus lifestyle and a direction in this life that is more suitable to our desires. By living the life we want, we silence the cost of following Jesus. It is important to keep in mind that redefining Him does not change Him. Jesus is the same yesterday, today, and forever. We need a clarion call to return to the historical Jesus found in the Gospels. A new revolution must rise that stirs up desire to live the life that this Jesus called us to live. We must understand that this Jesus will cost us. But again, remember that we are going to lose our lives no matter what. Either we lose our lives in the call to get out of the boats and follow, or we live as we want and lose it later when we stand before Him. May our choice line up with His call for us.

TAKING THE CHAPTER A BIT FURTHER

1. Why do you believe it is necessary for mankind to reinvent Jesus?
2. What specific advantages occur when we reinvent Jesus?
3. Why is it so hard for us to simply take Jesus at His Word and live it?

Chapter 14

How Can There Be a Cost in This No Cost America?

DEFINING THE COST

In trying to define the cost of anything, we can find results all over the spectrum. For example, what is the value of something? If there is a surplus of oil, gas prices are low. The need may drive it somewhat, but the quantity overrides it. If there is a decline in availability of oil, gas prices increase, and the demand becomes rather intense. It still costs to produce and transport it, but the price can fluctuate. So, what really is the value of something? That answer is not an easy one. What is the true depth of the cost of following Jesus? That again can fluctuate based on the person, era, environment, society, and the threat of spiritual expansion. Again, the true cost can be hard to discover.

For example, what is the true cost of following Jesus today? Ask a person living in the Bible Belt of the United States, a person living in New England, and a person living in Nigeria. The specifics of each answer will vary, but the fact of the cost will remain the same. There is either a cost to follow Jesus, or there is not. Culture and circumstances may cause the cost to vary, but the cost cannot both exist and not exist. Either mankind must pay a cost to follow, or the cost taught in Scripture is relative.

Interestingly, when you examine the idea of the cost of following Jesus, no passages seem to suggest a varying degree. There is just the plain text of Scripture, which continues to point us to a cost spoken of in both Jesus' teachings and all through the rest of the New Testament. The cost is more about the journey through which He transforms us into His image.

NO COST AMERICA

This brings us to the heart of this chapter. There is clearly a difference in daily cost in the United States as compared to most places in the world. Why is it so "easy" to follow here than in places of persecution? Does God just protect certain nations and not others? Does He simply keep some people safe from it while allowing others to face it regularly? Maybe we have not properly understood the cost.

It is easy to define the cost in places like Turkey. Christians cannot meet together and worship. They cannot share their faith, or they may be imprisoned. Christians cannot openly profess their faith, or they may be killed. If you come to Christ in Turkey, you could lose your job, your family, or even your life. The cost is clear and in your face daily.

However, in the United States, your faith for the most part can be openly displayed and broadcasted, and you can even attempt to share that faith with others. You can publicly carry your Bible, worship, pray, and spread the Word. So, where is the cost?

Many might find these next questions rather extreme, and when they first hear them, they might just suggest that the questions are inaccurate. Don't rush past them. Instead, take a few minutes to ponder them. Is it possible that the cost really is the same regardless of where you live? Is it possible that in some cases, the cost may actually be more severe in places where you believe it is the least? In other words, may it actually be harder to follow Jesus in places like the United States than in places with extreme persecution?

Please do not think for one moment that this is a suggestion that persecution in other nations is not hard and ruthless. Believers all over the world wake up daily to the pressures of following. Their cost is beyond the understanding of most of us. In that sense, there is no way we can even compare the costs. Would you rather live in America or in a country that hates Christians? There is no question that we would choose here in the United States. But before we conclude the matter, let's pause and wrestle a little further with that decision.

When a person follows Jesus in persecuted nations, what cost do they have to pay? For the most part, it is primarily a cost of their life and well-being. Again, that is not easy, and in no way do I suggest that it is. But the cost in America is the same. We just choose to only pay it in a smaller fashion. We claim to follow and give Him our lives, but we also regularly choose to live as we wish. There is little cost of following because we choose what we want over what He has taught us. Listen to these truths and put them in the present-day context of your life:

1. We are to carry our cross.
2. We are to hate our lives.
3. We are to forsake all.
4. We are not to lay up our treasures on this earth.
5. We are to seek first His kingdom.
6. We are to love Him with all our hearts.
7. We are to present our bodies a living sacrifice.
8. We are to esteem others better than ourselves.
9. We are to lay down our lives for others.
10. We are to share what we have with our brothers in need.

Obviously, in the moment, having a gun to our head while someone attempts to force us to deny Christ would be much harder than anything we face in the West. But in the long run, the pull of our hearts to follow Jesus in a soft way may be a greater temptation for us and may lead to false confessions and weak faith. America has been lulled to sleep by the materialism that we enjoy. By following in this manner, we have not only reinvented Jesus, but we have also poorly portrayed Him to a world that desperately needs Him. What makes this so scary is that there are many who will say that they follow, and when they stand before Him, they will find that He never knew them. A Jesus has been offered to the world that is neither saving nor sanctifying. He is a safe Jesus.

So is it wrong to live affluently when that lifestyle is available? Is it wrong to have the nice things we own? Is it wrong to enjoy this world and its pleasures as long as they are not inherently sin? As far as Scripture is concerned, this is not the problem. The problem does not come from having the things of the world. The problem comes from the way the world grabs our hearts, often so subtly that we are not paying attention when it happens. Additionally, when we compare ourselves with the multitude of believers around us, there appears to be little difference. We might wonder, why can't a believer have the best of both worlds? But remember Jesus' words, "What does it profit a man if he gains the world but loses his soul?" (Mark 8:36). Maybe we need to ask why we think it is possible to love God and the things of the world at the same time.

Just listen to the conversations that are front and center of those who profess faith and claim to be His followers. You will hear them discuss sports, weather, materialism, wealth, politics, pleasures, traveling, etc. Nothing is inherently wrong with these things. We need to be in this world. The problem is that far too many are so into the world that there is little difference between them and anyone around them.

And this is why it may actually be harder to live this cost in places such as the western countries than it is in areas where persecution is rampant. For example: believers in many persecuted areas have little of the world to pay other than their lives. They simply do not have anything else to give. In all actuality, affluent areas have many more treasures that could steal their hearts than the less affluent.

Keep in mind that in all cultures and civilizations, the call has always been the same. If you want to follow Jesus, it will cost you your life. The difference for affluent areas is that you not only have to give your life, but you must also let go of the world's goods. You cannot have that which could easily steal your heart. Is it possible to avoid letting it steal your heart? Yes, but remember what Jesus said: "It is easier for a camel to go through the eye of a needle than for a rich man to enter Heaven" (Mark 10:25). Those who qualify as rich men are most of the believers in the United States when compared with the world. Jesus emphasized that you cannot serve God and materialism. Therefore, living in affluent areas has more things to steal their hearts and more things to give up for cost.

THE LAODICEAN CHURCH

So how can a person who professes faith in a comfortable community truly pay a cost for following? What does that cost actually look like? In Revelation 2–3, Jesus discusses the status of seven different churches. It gives us great insight into how exactly Jesus feels about His church, His bride. The final church He discusses is the church of Laodicea. This will not be a complete and thorough study of that church or that passage. However, there are several important truths that must be examined:

1. Jesus is speaking to the church in Laodicea, which would imply genuine followers. A group of people meeting, even if they only claim faith, is not a church. This church had evidence that they were true followers.

2. They were a working church.
3. They were lukewarm, suggesting some small way of following.
4. Their struggle appears to be that they were rich and owned plenty of goods, having no need of anything. It certainly sounds much like the materialism in America.
5. They were putting their values in the wrong places. Their treasures were laid up on the earth.

The Laodicean church has some rather striking similarities with the church in America today, wouldn't you say? The two characteristics that seem to tie it all together are the materialism and the idea of not being in need of anything. This kind of mindset allows the church to become self-reliant instead of desperate for Him. Since we have so much to steal the desire of our hearts, we often do not hunger for Him. We can get what we want without Him. This is not so in many other areas of the world. They truly rely on Him for their daily existence. Giving up the things that could steal their hearts is not really much to sacrifice. To give up in affluency is to give up so much more, especially when we have been lured into believing we can have both the world and Jesus.

The American church does not realize it has slipped into a Laodicean mindset. We have accepted a soft way of life and we make little impact on our culture. We have chosen to blend in instead of confronting the sinful society we live in. We need to go back and look at Jesus and how He dealt with religiosity during that time and culture. He turned over the money tables and called out the religious crowd. But He also sent His followers into the world to call people to repent and change their ways. He never told His followers to just blend in and hope others ask about Him. He sent them forth as sheep in the midst of wolves. They knew what He expected of them, and they did it. Today, we believe He has sent us to just be in the world and make a soft impact. Be kind. Be loving. Be gentle. Hope that they will see the light in us. My friends, the light is so dim in many that there is no way anyone will be attracted to it. There needs to be serious change in our walk if we are going to make any difference in this pagan world. We need to revisit the historical Jesus.

HOW TO LIVE THE COST IN AN EASY SOCIETY

There is no question that one can live what Jesus and the New Testament taught in any society and in any given situation. I do not believe in situational ethics where the circumstances dictate our actions. Truth is truth, and obedience is obedience. There are no gimmicks or caveats that control following Christ as He expects. So, how do we live it in the ease and comforts of our world as we have it? There are three tests that draw this out for us. These tests work in any culture but are more difficult in an area where plenty can steal our hearts.

Test #1: Does He have your time?

We have all been given 24 hours or 1,440 minutes or 86,400 seconds a day. That is absolutely enough time to do all that He desires for us to do in a day. We often say that we do not have enough time to get something done. That may be true for the things that we want to do, but it is absolutely false for the plans He has for us. The reason why we struggle to accomplish the tasks He desires for us is we often fill our time with what we want over what He wants. There lies the battle between His kingdom and ours.

Have you ever evaluated your time and how you use it? If we are to give account for every idle word that we speak on the day of judgment (Matt 12:36), then what about every idle minute? Can a person truly live every second for God? I'm sure we would love to be able to do that, but just because it is far reaching does not mean we shouldn't give ample effort. How passionate are we about God? Undoubtedly, if we have more things to grab our time, then letting go of those things for the Kingdom will cost us.

Test #2: Does He have your talents?

Most people have multiple talents that enable them to do many interesting and important things. Have you ever stopped to consider all the talents you have been blessed with? Talents to do things for the Kingdom and God's programs. Talents to reach a world that is desperately in need of Jesus. Talents that are often wasted on one's personal passions.

So, take a moment and evaluate how you are talented. You are gifted. You have abilities to do things and to do them well. Here is the question: with the talents that you have, how are you using them for the Kingdom as opposed to your own interests? How are your talents being used to lay up treasure in Heaven in comparison to your own personal treasures? As we all know, there are no U-Hauls following hearses. We cannot take anything with us, so why then do we spend so much time and talent on things that will all burn?

Test #3: Does He have your treasures?

These three all tie together but need to be looked at separately as we have been doing. The time and talents we have are often used to build up our treasures. We put time into things that generate money, which generates more things. When it is all over, what then becomes of the things? All these do is grab our hearts. It is evident why our Lord warned us so much about our hearts and our treasures.

Does this mean we should not have anything? No house, cars, retirement, or things of any sort? Are we to hold onto nothing since it is true that anything could grab our hearts? The problem is rarely in the things that we may or may not have. The issue is always if they have us. One thing is clear: the less we have, the less of a chance there is that something can grab our hearts. That again is why some of the persecuted Christians find it easier to pay the cost because they own so little that has any chance of grabbing their hearts.

Take some time to evaluate what God has entrusted to you. We are all simply stewards since He is the owner of whatever may be registered to us. Our houses, cars, jobs, money—everything is all owned by our Master. We do not own these things, so why hold on to them so tightly? Just consider the issue of tithing. This is not the place to debate the word or the amount, but ask if you consider yourself someone who gives and whether that giving comes with some element of sacrifice. Is there any sacrifice involved in your time, talents, or treasures? Does He truly own it all, or are you in charge, and He simply comes along for the ride?

SOMETHING TO THINK ABOUT

We often tend to measure by the external and not look at the heart as God teaches us to do. These things that far too many of us hold dear are fleeting in this life. We each have only one life, and it will soon be over. Only what we do for eternal values and His glory will have eternal benefit. So why would we want to spend so much time, talent, and treasures on that which in the end will simply be wood, hay, and stubble? If we stood before God today and offered Him our time, talents, and treasures, would they have His praise? How do we keep the right balance?

When the apostles were called to follow, they had many of the same questions that perplex us now. They also heard Jesus say the same things we have heard in Scripture, and they personally saw Him live it out before their eyes. They learned to follow His model to the last detail. Here we are, 2,000 or so years later, with much concern over whether we are listening or being deceived. Sad to say for many that this will only be clear when they stand before Him.

There are several distinct passages in the Bible that describe us standing before Him one day. Romans 14:10–12 states that we will all stand before the judgement seat of Christ and give account of our lives. The same basic truth is also taught in 2 Corinthians 5:10. We will all appear before the judgement seat of Christ and have to give account of things done in the body, whether good or bad. 1 Corinthians 3 offers more insight as Paul teaches that everything we have done will be evaluated to see if it has eternal value or not. We know that this day is coming, and we will give account of what we have done. Wouldn't it be wise to be sure that when that day comes, you have lived in such a way as to hear His commendation? Or will you be ashamed at His appearing (1 John 2:28)?

We know that there will be no judgment for sin for those who are Christians. Romans 8 makes it clear that there is no condemnation ahead for the believer. Our sins have been atoned for so that they will be held against us no more. Praise God for that. However, that does not mean that we live our lives any way we want and for whatever purpose we want. Have we forgotten we have been bought and that our lives are not our own? Therefore, we are to glorify God with our lives and our bodies, which are His. How is our present lifestyle a picture of that calling? Are we any different from the rich man that had so much, he had to build more barns to house what he owned?

So, do we have to just give everything away and live in communes as paupers or vagabonds or nomads? Not remotely. *The call for the follower is simply to follow completely.* What that looks like for you and me could be different. His call for each of us is His personal call and His personal right to us. We know that this life is not ours to live, but His. His call, His kingdom, and His plan. Not ours. With all that we have and with all that captivates our time and energy, how do we make our lives even come close to resembling what Scripture calls us to? We have to answer that in some way before we stand before Him and give account of our lives.

TAKING THE CHAPTER A BIT FURTHER

1. List some ways it is possible to live in affluence and still have a hunger for God.
2. Why is it that the things of the world are not compatible with the heart for God?
3. How can one be in the world and not of the world? Study John 17 to see.

Chapter 15

In the World and Not of the World

One of the most argued phrases among the Christian community might well be the one that Jesus gave regarding being in the world and not of the world. Here are a few places where He taught that.

1. Matthew 28:19—"go into the world"
2. John 15:19—"not of the world"
3. John 17:14–16—"not of the world" (3 times)
4. John 17:18—"I also have sent them into the world"
5. John 20:21—"I also send you" [into the world]
6. 1 John 4:4–6—a comparison of those who are in the world and those who are of God

In these verses alone, Jesus and John make it clear that we are not of this world, but we are to go into the world. That teaching has generated all sorts of discussions among believers! For example, during my college years, my roommate argued with me that young Christians should not engage in "mixed bathing"; he firmly believed girls and boys should not be allowed to swim at the same time. He felt that this was an example of being in the world and not of it. Some believers say that a Christian man should not have long hair. This was argued heavily in the 1960s and 70s during the hippie movement. They felt that long hair meant that the man was conforming to the standards of the world. Similar to that argument is the position that women should not cut their hair, and some also argue that women should not wear makeup or jewelry.

Growing up in a conservative Christian home, I experienced my parents setting numerous "Sabbath" restrictions for us, such as no traveling on Sunday, no eating out on Sunday, and no television on Sunday. Vacations were taken after midnight on Sunday so that travel would be in compliance with their rules. We also always returned before the next Sunday.

Of course, there is the ever-popular argument about music. Certain videos posted online explain why believers should not listen to or sing with church music that comes from certain other churches. There are good people on all sides of this. The whole contemporary Christian music movement is still a raging debate. Some have concluded that the music before worship is more like a rock concert than a worship time. Some churches have even used secular music as their song set in the morning worship service. Is the culture conforming the church, or is the church conforming the culture? The debate rages on.

It is important to understand why this debate even exists. Giving people the benefit of the doubt, it's best to conclude that they are trying to understand and apply the teachings of Jesus that say we are to be in the world but not of the world. Christians are trying to be relevant in this pagan world while at the same time trying to be godly. If anyone thinks this is an easy stance, they obviously have not discussed it on a deeper level.

CONTRADICTIONS

The contradictions believers consistently apply to the idea of being in the world and not of the world are rather alarming. Some believers argue that suggesting Santa Claus on any level is purely Satanic, but they do Easter egg hunts. Some believers teach that alcohol is evil and of the world, but they attend sporting events and willingly pass it down to the people next to them. Some believers conclude that obeying the government is a mandate but see no real problem with speeding. To be consistent in our conclusions is not easy.

Part of the reason for this is the fact that the Bible offers very few clear illustrations of what exactly Jesus meant by being in the world and not of the world. If Jesus had just given us a few examples, we could maybe apply this teaching more readily. The ambiguity of the Bible on this theme makes us wonder about clear application. However, there are some biblical guidelines that can be useful in our quest for understanding.

God clearly wants us in the world. He does not teach that He wants us living in some communal area far away from everyone else. He sent us into the world. Yet how do we avoid the world getting into us? That is part of the cost of living for Christ in a world that lies in the hands of the wicked one. Satan is the god of this world, and if we are not careful, we will be conformed to it.

AN OLD TESTAMENT LOOK AT SEPARATION

Adam and Eve

The idea of separation actually begins in the Garden of Eden. When God made man and put him on this huge planet called Earth, He actually placed man in a restricted area—the first "gated community" if you will—called the Garden of Eden. The Garden of Eden was man's dwelling place, not likely the entire world. Genesis 2:8 states that God planted a garden and set man inside. However, in Genesis 1:28, man is told to replenish the earth. Regardless of God's intent, man sinned and was kicked out of the Garden, driven out by God as stated in Genesis 3:23. And by chapter 4, man began to move all over the earth.

Noah

Separation becomes more clear with Noah as only he and his family were given grace to endure. The entire world had become corrupt before God, and He spared Noah and his family only. The ark became a place of separation. This separation, of course, was not necessarily a separation from the world but a separation from the judgment on the world. The people of the world would not be able to get to Noah and his family. They were clearly separated from the ark. Noah and his family learned what it meant to be in the world (positionally) but not of the world (relationally).

When those on the ark exited, they were the only living people on the earth. All the rest of mankind had been judged by God and killed. God then told Noah and his family to replenish the earth. Noah and his family had the entire earth to inhabit. There does not seem to be any teaching on actual physical separation on any level. Think about this: how were they to understand being a follower of God without allowing the world to influence them?

Tower of Babel

Genesis 11:1 says that the whole earth was of one language and speech. How many actual people were on the earth is not clear, and neither is the expanse of mankind. Man was roaming the earth. As they journeyed, they stopped at the land of Shinar and dwelt there. At this location, they decided to build a tower that would reach into heaven. There are numerous opinions as to why they wanted to build this tower, but since the text does not explicitly explain why, maybe it is best to just leave as is. One thing we can be certain of: God told them to replenish the earth, but they wanted to build a tower that would act as a central location, which would limit any spreading. Apparently, man was defying God's order to spread out.

At that point in time, there did not seem to be any concerns about separation. As a matter of fact, just the opposite might have been the inclination. God appears to have wanted mankind to populate the whole earth and move forward. Obviously, this is in light of the fact that He was about to choose one man and one people that would carry His name into all the world.

Abraham to the End of Genesis

In Genesis 12 God calls a man by the name of Abram, giving specific directions that Abram should "Get thee out of thy country, and from thy kindred, and from thy father's house, unto a land that I will show thee" (Gen 12:1, KJV). Here, separation is obviously stated. "Get thee out of . . . and from" means to separate. Also, God was going to send them to a particular land that was to be theirs and theirs alone. Separation from the world now would be the norm for His children.

God makes the distinction clear to Abram and promises to be his God, stating that his descendants were to be uniquely His people. All the world would be blessed by this one nation, and if anyone blessed this nation, God would bless them. If anyone cursed this nation, God would curse them. There is no question that God's people were beginning to see it would be them against the world.

As you continue through Genesis, you can see that God's people are truly a distinct people in a distinct land. There are times when they are compromised to either permit foreign connections or to even travel outside the land. Here are a few examples:

1. Genesis 12:7—God tells Abram that He will give to him the land where he is presently, and yet, in verse 10 Abram heads to Egypt. Needless to say, it does not end well. God's people were not to be in Egypt.

2. Genesis 13—Abram and Lot separate over their herds. That does not go well for Lot and nearly costs him everything. God's people were to be together and not compromised in the world like Sodom and Gomorrah.
3. Genesis 14—Abram rescues Lot and returns him to his family. God's people are back together as one and separated from all others.
4. Genesis 15–27—There are minimal travels within the boundaries of the land, but in Genesis 27:43, Jacobs flees to Haran, the original place where God called Abram to leave (separate) and go to the land God had for him.
5. Genesis 27–37—This primarily covers the exchanges between Jacob and Esau, but in chapter 37, a major turn of events occurs.
6. Genesis 37—Joseph is sold as a slave and ends up in Egypt.
7. Genesis 37–50—This describes the many stories connected to Joseph and his brothers, with all of God's people eventually arriving in Egypt. Again, keep in mind that this was never to be the place of their residency.

God's People in Egypt

As time went on in Israel, the idea of separating from the world (Egypt) became even more apparent. It all began with the land that Israel was given. They were to be given any land that they wanted, and they chose to live in Goshen. It would seem that they lived in that area of Egypt apart from the Egyptians. God's people were separated from Egypt even while they lived there. This became important to them later on.

Eventually, in Exodus, God begins to plague Egypt as part of His plan to punish that nation and expose their false gods. However, the land of Goshen where Israel lived, separated from Egypt and the world, was spared these plagues. Now, it is not clear if the first three plagues were kept out of Goshen, but it is explicitly stated in Exodus 8:22 that the fourth plague of flies did not occur where Israel dwelt. God was making a distinction between His people and the world. This action became the first very clear separation of being in the world and not of the world in the Scriptures.

The following plagues reveal a continued separation between God's people and the people of the world (Gen. 9:4–6, 9:26, 10:23, and of course, the death angel if Israel applied the blood). Was God just protecting His people, or was He also beginning to teach them the principle of being in the world but not of the world? It is also fascinating that the plagues seemed to attack the gods of Egypt. Once again, we are not of this world, and maybe this part of Scripture shows more of that emphasis.

The Law of Separation

Once Israel left Egypt in the direction of the Promised Land, they began to accept more of their distinctiveness and specialty as a people. This truth became more obvious when God gave them the Law whereby He made it bountifully clear that they were to be different from the world around them. He would be their God, and they were to have no other gods before Him. He even gave them specific actions to take regarding the world around them. A few commandments about separation are found in the following verses:

1. Exodus 19:5–6—They were to be a peculiar people unto Him alone.
2. Exodus 23:20–33—God's people alone were to dwell in the Promised Land.
3. Exodus 31:12–17—The Sabbath was a unique sign only between God and His people.
4. Exodus 33:16—They must be separate from all the peoples of the world.
5. Leviticus 11—There must be separation of what animals were clean and unclean.
6. Leviticus 11:39–40—This was the law of being unclean if they touched a dead animal.
7. Leviticus 11:41–47—They had dietary laws of separation.
8. Leviticus 20:24—They needed to be separated from all the peoples of the earth.
9. Leviticus 20:26—They were set apart from the nations to be His own.
10. Deuteronomy 7:3—They could not marry anyone outside of their people.

Without any ambiguity, God told Israel that they were to be His people, and He would be their God. They were to live separate from the world with their own laws, regulations, and leadership. This relationship was a personal one between the Creator God and the chosen people, Israel. They would be uniquely His and refrain from associations with the world.

God's People and the Promised Land

When the people eventually arrived at the Promised Land, they were told by God to totally clean out the land. In other words, no one could live in the land that was called Israel except for the people of God. Total separation was not just an idea; it was a command.

Actually, God began to tell them this even before they entered the land. In Deuteronomy 12, He explains that they needed to wipe out the people and their gods. Deuteronomy 12:2 tells them to "utterly destroy." God uses the same phrase in Deuteronomy 20:17, and He even names everyone whom His people had to utterly destroy.

Then, when they entered the land, they were told again explicitly not to leave one person alive. Joshua 1:5 states that not one man would be able to stand against them. Joshua 6:21 says that they utterly destroyed all that was in the city of Jericho, and Joshua 8:24 records that they slayed all the inhabitants of Ai. This was exactly what God had told them to do.

Just a side note here: God's orders and Israel's actions can seem pretty unfair to us now. Exterminate an entire people? But we need to remember that these people were extremely wicked, and they wanted to influence Israel to fall away from the Lord. Israel was His nation, and this was their land. Yes, this is not a completely satisfactory answer, but keep in mind that His ways are above our ways. There are things about God that we will never understand, and if we had a God we could understand completely, would He be God at all?

Anyway, when we get to Judges, we find that Israel didn't drive out the inhabitants as God had told them to do. In numerous places in the first chapter, tribe after tribe failed to remove everyone from the land. Therefore, these enemies became thorns in the side of God's people. Sure enough, they led Israel astray into idol worship, just as the Lord had predicted. They went from being in the world and not of the world to being completely immersed in the world and its doings.

Throughout the rest of the Old Testament, there is constant tension in God's people over being in this world and not of the world. They wanted to be like all the other nations in every way. All the other nations had a king, so they wanted a king. They latched on to the gods that surrounded them in the pagan nations. They made alliances with foreign nations to fight battles in direct violation of His laws. God desired for Israel to remain separate from the world, but by the end of the Old Testament, His people were in shambles. Finally, for 400 years, God went silent, speaking nothing new through His prophets and apparently just waiting. What He was really doing, however, was preparing His people for the Messiah.

JESUS AND SEPARATION

Jesus spoke to a predominantly Jewish audience with Old Testament roots. So while He taught that we should be in this world, but not of this world, he did not spend too much time explaining it. One, the New Testament priority at that time was still the nation of Israel, which was to remain separate. Second, He was laying the foundation for the church, which would receive a whole different message about being in the world and not of the world.

The question that we must ponder is what exactly does Jesus mean by this? How can one be in the world and not of the world? This is of major importance for the believers as we try to impact this world without being like the world. How did Jesus accomplish it?

It Was Not Outward

As best as we can discern, Jesus looked like a regular guy living in the Holy Land. He had the same outward clothing, a beard, and probably a reasonable length of hair. Not once in the Gospels is there a mention of Jesus' attire and whether He stood out or just blended in. You can be sure if He was not fitting in outwardly, the Pharisees or someone else in religious leadership would have called Him out.

There is no reference anywhere to any indecency. The only time where it comes into question is on the cross. Debate has raged for years over whether He was naked on the cross, but other than that, there does not appear to be any concern at any time about His care of His clothing. Since He was a Rabbi and, of course, God, it can be strongly assumed that He was always modest in attire.

Nowhere does Jesus even address clothing, hair, or facial hair. Interestingly, these often seem to be major subjects of discussion today for the church whereas Jesus spoke nothing on this subject. Either it was not much of an issue in His day, or maybe we have made more of it than we should. Because of other Scriptures, it is safe to conclude that modesty was in order for His attire.

It Was Not His Environment

Today, we hear that believers should not visit certain places. It does not appear that Jesus had exactly the same standard. Now, we would be amiss to conclude that He went to some of the seedier places in towns. Some cities certainly were worse. At no time did Jesus hang out with a crowd or company that made His association with them demonstrate He was partaking with them.

We know prostitutes existed in that day, but if there was a local hangout, Jesus was not found there. Prostitutes came to Him, but it does not seem like He ever went to any known places of immoral behavior. He was accused of eating with the publicans and sinners, but did He ever just hang out with them to be with them? He never taught anything that suggested there were places you should or should not attend. These points of discussion do not seem to be at the heart of Jesus' teachings on being in the world and not of the world. In addition, it does not appear He gave much detail to explain His teaching. He just seems to have made the statements that we are not of this world. What did He mean by that? I suspect His main purpose was to emphasize that following Him would even cost us the world we lived in. We will be tempted to make this world our home, but we must remember that we are just passing through.

The Scriptures Teach We Would Be Hated

It's sobering to think of the many times Jesus taught that we would be hated in this world. Just think through these few examples:

1. Matthew 10:22—hated of all men
2. Matthew 24:9—delivered to be persecuted (possibly Tribulation)
3. James 4:4—loving the world and an enemy of God
4. 1 John 3:3—hated by the world
5. 1 John 4:4–6—a clear difference of those of the world and not of the world

Let's pause here a bit. Scripture teaches that we are not of this world as Jesus is not of this world. Yet we are to be sent into the world. Scripture also teaches that we will be hated and persecuted because we are not of this world. But for many who follow Christ, especially in the West, they experience little to no persecution and rarely any hatred. So, we must ask ourselves one question: Why so little persecution and hatred, at least outward hatred?

Sadly, at least some of the answer lies in the fact that we are both *in* and *of* the world. We want the best of all worlds. If we live like nonbelievers, we won't face the world's hatred. It's easy.

Yet God calls us to be different. We have to come to grips that when we surrendered to Him, our lives ended. His life in us began on that day. And this will bring us into direct opposition with the world and its view. Our biblical worldview is not of this world. Our biblical worldview will cause us to be not of this world. Our biblical worldview will cause us to be hated.

Take for example one simple discussion on marriage. A biblical worldview says that marriage is one woman and one man for life. Now, let that play out at the water coolers or in university dining halls. Does anyone think that that statement won't face any attack? The world hates this view and wants us to embrace and condone its view. Believers can do neither. Hence, we will be hated.

TAKING THE CHAPTER A BIT FURTHER

1. Describe how Jesus was in the world and not of the world.
2. Read through the Book of Acts and point out examples where the followers were in the world and not of the world.
3. How can you live this way today? List some practical examples.

Chapter 16

No Pain, No Gain—Are You Willing to Pay the Cost?

When we look back on our lives and evaluate our journey with Jesus, what about that journey will be most important to us? Will it be how comfortable life has been for us? Will it be how easy it has been for us to follow Christ? Will it be how little cost we paid on this journey?

There is no need to rush out and look for ways to be persecuted. The emphasis of this book is not simply suffering for suffering's sake, but on losing one's life for Jesus in whatever way that may look like. The challenge is for us to fall more in love with Jesus than we do the world. Looking at the church of America, can anyone truly say that the message of cost and loving God supremely over self and pleasures is how we are living the faith? How much of your life is consumed with Jesus?

There is a saying popular among the gym rats and other fitness gurus: "No pain, no gain." Their point is that if any of us want to meet weight and fitness goals, it will cost us. It will cost us our food. It will cost us our indulgences. It will cost us time, energy, and pleasures. It will cost us our all if we take it seriously. We can give a half-hearted effort and gain some progress, but truth be told, if there is no pain, there will be no gain.

Before we make the transition into the spiritual application, let's deflect an oft repeated claim that says we cannot do this because it has to be God. It is true that without Him, we can do nothing. But nowhere in Scripture does it teach that we are to sit idly by and have no role in the sanctification process. We are, in fact, to be actively involved.

Maybe Philippians 2:12–13 can clarify this for us. It tells us we must "work out your own salvation with fear and trembling" (vs 12). In other words, we must be active in living out our faith and doing the proper things for spiritual growth. We should make time to dive into the Word, pray, and practice other spiritual disciplines as it is our responsibility. Then, verse 13 adds, "for it is God that works in you, both to will and to do of His good pleasure."

Yes, it is all God who receives glory, honor, and praise. Yes, it is God who works in us. Yes, we cannot do anything without Him. However, He works in us while we actively cooperate on the journey. His will shall still be done. We will one day be like Him, but the journey has two possibilities. One, we take the path where we work in harmony with Him. Two, we choose the path where we resist Him, and He then does His work in stronger ways, including discipline and pruning. The end result is the same. The process, however, is not. How we mature, grow, and journey will be up to our obedience and actions. The goal we should live by daily is that when He calls us home, there is not much left to do in us to make us like Jesus. We have been conformed on such a deep level that Christ is truly shining through. May we be as passionate about His likeness as we are of the world's comforts.

Here is where the pain comes in. We can go to the fitness gym, work off 500 calories, and leave with a sense of accomplishment. The trainer did his job. He pushed us, and now upon leaving, we have decisions to make. Stop at the donut shop? Drive through McDonalds? Go eat some yogurt? Choices made on a daily basis have longer lasting fruit than just the moments in the gym. This is why many do not have victory with weight loss or getting into shape. They are not willing to pay the cost.

Jesus has called us to the cost of following Him. It involves getting out of the boat (or wherever He calls us from) and staying out of the boat as we continue on with Him. We will long to go back. It is our sinful desire and will to do so. Yet, we must realize that this life is not ours to live. We get out of the boat and say to ourselves, "So long." We die when our feet hit the shore, and we stay dead until one day, He takes us home to enjoy the pleasures of Heaven. We are dead, and our lives are hidden with Christ in God.

Staying dead is the hard part. This is where the pain comes in. But we want to have one thing and to do another and to go there and be this and enjoy that and so on. We want to live for Jesus in the general sense of the word but not too fanatically. We still want to enjoy this life and all it has to offer. We want the best of both worlds. But no pain, no gain.

The call to walk in this fashion will cost us. It means we cannot do what others seem to be able to do and go where others seem to go. We cannot live a life of a soft Jesus. We need to truly evaluate our lives and whether there is any cost for following Jesus at all. Far too many American followers of Jesus have chosen to blend into the world and be part of it while also holding onto Jesus. At some point we have to ask if maybe this lifestyle we choose is a bad representation of the true Jesus of the New Testament. We need to stop being conformed to this world and set out daily to be a transformer of this world. The world needs to see authentic faith, not a mere phony picture of Him. For many, the only difference in us and them is that we go to church or in some way act a little like Jesus. We are either all in or not. Being all in will cost us.

People are dying and going to hell daily. Only authentic faith has any chance of catching their attention so they can begin to see the true Jesus. That means confronting sin more than just ignoring sin. God's people have always spoken out about Him and His standards. American faith has almost forgotten that. We have silently ignored the sins of abortion, alcohol abuse, drug abuse, pornography, and attacks on marriage. As the saying goes, all it takes for evil to prevail is for good people to do nothing. We are not merely interested in changing a culture but impacting souls one at a time. It means more of a concerted effort to engage this world and the lostness of it. It means being willing to pay whatever price necessary to be salt and light. It means no longer living a safe and soft Jesus. It is time for the church to be the church and stop placating the world—to be in this world but determine not to be of it.

And this is where it just may be harder to live the Christian life in a place of affluence. There is more to say no to. We have more things pulling at our hearts. We have more potential loves than just God. We have more options in our day than just living for Him. We have more battles to wage every day.

This is truly a life worth living. It is truly worth whatever sacrifice we may make. Living a cost-filled life for Jesus is so worth whatever we may miss out on this side. He is entirely worth it. But the greatest gain in the end is Jesus. We will never be sorry for any pain that helps us become more like Him. Let me conclude this chapter with an article written in the early 1900s by the Wesleyan pastor, G.D. Watson. What he says sums it up so well:

> If God has called you to be really like Jesus, He will draw you into a life of crucifixion and humility, and put upon you such demands of obedience, that you will not be able to follow other people, or measure yourself by other Christians, and in many ways He will seem to let other good people do things which He will not let you do.

Other Christians and ministers who seem very religious and useful, may push themselves, pull wires, and work schemes to carry out their plans, but you cannot do it; and if you attempt it, you will meet with such failure and rebuke from the Lord as to make you sorely penitent.

Others may boast of themselves, of their work, of their success, of their writings, but the Holy Spirit will not allow you to do any such thing, and if you begin it, He will lead you into some deep mortification that will make you despise yourself and all your good works.

Others may be allowed to succeed in making money, or may have a legacy left to them, but it is likely God will keep you poor, because He wants you to have something far better than gold, namely, a helpless dependence on Him, that He may have the privilege of supplying your needs day by day out of an unseen treasury.

The Lord may let others be honored and put forward, and keep you hidden in obscurity, because He wants you to produce some choice, fragrant fruit for His coming glory, which can only be produced in the shade. He may let others be great, but keep you small. He may let others do a work for Him and get the credit for it, but He will make you work and toil on without knowing how much you are doing; and then to make your work still more precious, He may let others get the credit for the work which you have done, and thus make your reward ten times greater then Jesus comes.

The Holy Spirit will put a strict watch over you, with a jealous love, and will rebuke you for little words and feelings, or for wasting your time, which other Christians never seem distressed over. So make up your mind that God is an infinite Sovereign, and has a right to do as He pleases with His own. He may not explain to you a thousand things which puzzle your reason in His dealings with you, but if you absolutely sell yourself to be His love slave, He will wrap you up in a jealous love, and bestow upon you many blessings which come only to those who are in the inner circle.

Settle it forever, then, that you are to deal directly with the Holy Spirit, and that He is to have the privilege of tying your tongue, or chaining your hand, or closing your eyes, in ways that He does not seem to use with others. Now when you are so possessed with the loving God that you are, in your secret heart, pleased and delighted over this peculiar, personal, private, jealous guardianship and management of the Holy Spirit over your life, you will have found the vestibule of Heaven.

So how do we die to this world and self? We need a fresh surrender of our will and our all. It begins with a genuine prayer of repentance for the past, self-willed life. Then, give a serious evaluation of all you have—time, talent, and treasures. Begin giving Him control of these areas of your life bit by bit as He shows these to you. Remind yourself daily that this is not your life to live. This life you have is His life in and through you. As you maintain this walk, in prayer and Scripture, you will see Him reveal the steps ahead. May we follow the true Jesus and live a life resembling His call for His glory.

Our life of self must die. We must come to the place where it is no longer I, but Christ. He must permeate all we do, say, and own. If your life is not all about Christ, then what is it? If you have completed this book, there must be some kind of hunger in you to be like Jesus. Go for it. Don't let the love of the world grab your heart. You are going to lose your life one way or another. Either lose your life now so you can find it in Christ or live your life now for self and lose it when you stand before Him. So, what will it be?

TAKING THE CHAPTER A BIT FURTHER

1. Why is it so hard to live for Jesus?
2. If He has given us all things that pertain to life and godliness, why do we struggle so to live in victory?
3. What one thing in your life would it be painful to surrender to God because you know the pain of it would be difficult? Why is that so?

Chapter 17

Why Are Many Not Willing to Pay the Cost?

IF YOU CAREFULLY EXAMINE the Gospels where Jesus met with people who were interested in following Him, you will see that many of them encountered personal conflicts that impacted their decisions. For some, it was the pull of the world. For others, it was the emergency of the day. And some couldn't see why it would be a priority. Those conflicts all boiled down to one thing: those that wouldn't follow simply did not love Him with all their heart.

Love, however, is the one truth that sets Christianity apart from all other religions. God so loved that He gave His Son. Jesus so loved that He gave His life. Jesus taught of love and lived a life of love. He told His disciples that it would be the one mark that defined them. Even later in history, the writers emphasized the importance of love. Love has always been the qualifier of the true follower of Jesus. That is why Jesus said it summed up the Law. Let's study this thought further throughout Scripture.

LAW IN THE OLD TESTAMENT

When people study the Old Testament and God's children, they tend to focus on the tenets of the Law. The Law seems to be the centerpiece of all that surrounds God's people. It is true that when He put Adam and Eve in the Garden of Eden, they had to obey. It is true what when He called men to follow Him, He gave them specifics of obedience such as build an ark or sacrifice a son. Then, when the people were two million strong and heading back to the Promised Land, they received the Law from Him. We are most familiar with the 10 commandments, but there are many more commandments included in Exodus through Deuteronomy. All of these were aimed at helping His people to be separated from the world.

Even prior to the commandment to remember the Sabbath day and keep it holy, God had required a special Sabbath day. On the seventh day of creation, He rested. Scripture also teaches on the Sabbath regarding picking up the manna as Israel headed to the Promised Land. In Exodus 16 (several chapters before the Law was given), God gave Israel the manna to sustain them throughout their journey. However, He established clear guidelines. They were to pick up only the amount needed for themselves and their families. They were also to pick up extra on the sixth day so that they would have enough on the seventh, the Sabbath Day. Clearly, before the Law, God had been commanding His people to obey Him.

Therefore, it is impossible to study the Old Testament and the relationship between God and His people without discussing the Law. He called His people to follow and obey Him. However, to only study the Law and miss out on His teaching about loving Him would do a great disservice to the call of God given to His people. He had no interest in blind obedience. He had no desire for His people to be box checkers. He wanted a relationship with them that flowed out of a heart of love for Him.

LOVE IN THE OLD TESTAMENT

The first time *love* occurs as a word in the Old Testament is Genesis 22. Now, the law of the first occurrences is often a hint of something bigger in the Bible; the theme goes from a mere hint in the first place it appears to a huge concept as the Bible unfolds, one that can take a lifetime to unpack. In Genesis 22:2, God gives us one of these "first occurrences"— the word and action of love—in the story of a father and a son. Not just any son, but the "beloved" son of the father. Yet this father was willing to sacrifice his child as an obedient action to the call of God. This story of Abraham and Isaac is full of parallels to the one about the Father and the Son found in the New Testament. God was clearly sending a message to His people of the true Father and Son relationship that He desires to have with them. It would be based on the truth of love.

As the Old Testament continues, love is threaded in the stories of the followers of the one true God:

1. Genesis 24:67—Isaac loved Rebekah.
2. Genesis 25:28—Isaac loved Esau.
3. Genesis 25:28—Rebekah loved Jacob.
4. Genesis 29:20—Jacob served seven years for Rachel and his love for her.
5. Genesis 37:3—Jacob loved Joseph.
6. Genesis 44:20—Jacob loved Benjamin

These are just some of the examples of love in the Old Testament prior to the Law. The idea is very clear here in these verses; God was highlighting the importance of love in relationships as a picture of what He desires for Himself and His people. As they saw this love lived out, they could relate to their Father, God.

In addition to these pictures, God also began to weave the teaching of love into His Law. He did not want a people consisting of puppets blindly obeying him. Obedience is truly important, but the heart of obedience is even more so. Look at these verses and see how love was the foundation of their obedience:

1. Exodus 20:5–6—Right in the middle of the 10 commandments, God includes both truths of love and hate. It has always been one or the other. There is no middle ground with God. You either love and obey Him, or you hate Him. Those who bow down to other gods are those who hate Him (v. 5). Those who keep His commandments are those who love Him (v. 6). That theme of loving and keeping His commandments resonates all throughout Scripture.
2. Leviticus 19:18, 34—Love your neighbor.
3. Deuteronomy 4:37—God chose Israel because He chose to love them. He loved them first. Now, this love is what He desires for those who are His children. We love; therefore, we obey.
4. Deuteronomy 5:10—Love Him and keep His commands.
5. Deuteronomy 6:5—Love God with all . . .
6. Deuteronomy 7:9, 11:1, 13, 22—Love and then keep His commandments. That is His order for us. We love Him and out of our love for Him, we obey Him.
7. Deuteronomy 13:3—God tests us to know whether we love Him. Now, let's be clear. God is omniscient and knows this, so why does He give

us the test? We have to come to grips with our love for Him because unless we do, we will struggle with our obedience.

8. Deuteronomy 30:6, 16, 20—Same truths are seen here.
9. Joshua 22:5, 23:11—More of the same truths are also shown.

It is evident what God was doing. The Law defined the outward actions of those who followed Him. Even now, after the time of the Law, because we are His children, we ought to have a behavior consistent with our words. If we say it, then we ought to live it. However, if we only obey because we have to, then the obedience is simply a formality. It's a clear parent-child relationship, when you think about it. My earlier book on parenting teaches this as well, particularly regarding obedience. The key to this process is getting your child's heart. If you have their heart, the obedience is a natural outgrowth. We love; therefore, we obey. If we mess up that order, we will not have true obedience. True God-centered obedience starts with the theme of love first, and then out of that flows obedience.

JESUS TAUGHT LOVE WITH OBEDIENCE

We know that He loves us. We know He loved us first. This is all part of the relationship that He desires to have with us. He calls us to love Him out of His love for His children. Not only did He love us, but also He gave His life for us. He backed up that love with actions that truly demonstrated His love. On this foundation, He calls us to love Him and then obey Him.

A lawyer approached Jesus one day in order to tempt Him (Matt 22:35). He asked Jesus a question that he thought would corner Him: "Teacher, which is the great commandment in the law?" (Matt 22:36). This lawyer obviously hadn't read the book of Deuteronomy very carefully. He would have known the answer to that question.

Jesus kept his answer specific. He boiled it down to two things: Love God with all your heart, mind, and soul and love your neighbor as yourself. Of all the things that Jesus could have said, He directed the man's heart to the emotion of love. Why? Because it has always been God's desire for His people to love Him and *then* obey Him. That was true in the Old Testament, and it is certainly true in Jesus' teachings.

- John 14:15—"If you love Me, keep My commandments." Love is listed first.
- John 14:21—"He who has My commandments, and keeps them, it is he who loves Me." Again, love must be what comes before obedience.

- John 14:23—"If anyone loves Me, he will keep My Word." Once we love Him, then we will want to obey Him.
- John 14:24—"He who does not love Me does not keep my words." A lack of obedience is a sure sign of a lack of love for Him.
- John 15:10—"If you keep My commandments, you will abide in My love." Here, He affirms the order but also strengthens it as an ongoing component of obedience.
- John 15:14—"You are my friends, if you do whatever I command you." Now, the relationship is clear. We have this connection with God not because we do what He says but because our obedience flows out of a heart that is full of love towards God.

Remember the question that Jesus asked Peter when Peter had drifted back into fishing? Jesus asked Peter if he loved Him. Not "Peter do you do [whatever you want to put here]." Instead, it was "Peter, do you love Me?" Love was the question. It was the question in the Old Testament. It was the answer to the lawyer's question. It was the question given to Peter. God knows we can only obey Him when we love Him.

THE EPISTLES' TEACHING ON LOVE

Although the word *love* does not appear in Acts, one can readily see how the early followers loved one another. It was an attitude that began to define them. Chuck Swindoll, in his book *Hope Again*, relates the attitude very well:

> One of the most profound comments made regarding the early church came from the lips of a man named Aristides, sent by the Emperor Hadrian to spy out those strange creatures known as "Christians." Having seen them in action, Aristides returned with a mixed report. But his immortal words to the emperor have echoed down through history: "Behold! How they love one another."[1]

Swindoll also mentions the Christian leader Tertullian. In the latter part of the second century, Tertullian wrote a defense of Christian practice called the *Apologia*. After defending the church from false accusations, Tertullian went on to explain what Christians do and why they do it. In the following excerpt, he begins by talking about the church's use of money. What he says in chapter 39 of his *Apology* can be a bit surprising:

1. Swindoll, Charles. *Hope Again: When Life Hurts and Dreams Fade*. Thomas Nelson, 1997.

> There is no buying and selling of any sort in the things of God. Though we have our treasure-chest, it is not made up of purchase-money, as of a religion that has its price. On the monthly day, if he likes, each puts in a small donation; but only if it be his pleasure, and only if he be able: for there is no compulsion; all is voluntary. These gifts are, as it were, piety's deposit fund. For they are not taken thence and spent on feasts, and drinking-bouts, and eating-houses, but to support and bury poor people, to supply the wants of boys and girls destitute of means and parents, and of old persons confined now to the house; such, too, as have suffered shipwreck; and if there happen to be any in the mines, or banished to the islands, or shut up in the prisons . . . See, they say, how they love one another.

They loved others because they had met the God of love and had been changed by His love. The Epistles clearly demonstrate this change, as well. One way it appears is through the phrase "one another." The church began to be a living organism and a family. They belonged to one another. Therefore, God taught them to pray for one another, to encourage one another, to exhort one another, to bear one another's burdens, and so much more. There are at least 30 of these occurrences in the New Testament (see Appendix 4).

But the "one another" that is repeated the most is "love one another." While the others in the list occur once, this one appears at least 15 times (John 13:34, 13:35, 15:12,17; Romans 13:8, I Thessalonians 3:12, 4:9; I Peter 1:22; I John 3:11, 23, 4:7, 11, 12; and 2 John 5). God expects His followers to love one another, and that is only possible when we love Him. With that as the foundation, notice what the New Testament teaches about the Law.

1. Romans 13:10—"Love does no harm to a neighbor; therefore love *is* the fulfillment of the law."
2. Galatians 5:14—"For all the law is fulfilled in one word, *even* in this: "You shall love your neighbor as yourself."
3. James 2:8—"If you really fulfill *the* royal law according to the Scripture, "You shall love your neighbor as yourself," you do well."

These three Scriptures confirm exactly what the Old Testament and Jesus said. His order for us is intentional. We are to love Him, and out of that flows a love that is beyond human understanding or will. We love because He poured His love into us. John confirms that thought in 1 John as seen in each of the listed verses below:

- 1 John 2:3—"we know that we know Him, if we keep His commandments."

- 1 John 2:6—"He who says he abides in Him ought himself also to walk just as He walked."
- 1 John 2:9—"He who says He is in the light and hates his brother is in darkness."
- 1 John 2:10—"He who loves his brother abides in the light."
- 1 John 2:11—"He who hates his brother is in darkness."
- 1 John 2:15—"Do not love the world or the things in the world. If anyone loves the world, the love of the Father is not in him."
- 1 John 3:1—"Behold what manner of love the Father has bestowed on us."
- 1 John 3:16—"By this we know love, because He laid down His life for us. And we also ought to lay down our lives for the brethren."
- 1 John 3:17—"But whoever has this world's goods and sees his brother in need and shuts up his heart from him, how does the love of God abide in him?"
- 1 John 3:18—"Let us not love in word on in tongue, but in deed"
- 1 John 3:19—"And by this (doing verse 18) we know that we are of the truth."
- 1 John 3:20—"For if our heart condemns us not"
- 1 John 3:23—"This is His commandment that. . .we love one another."
- 1 John 3:24—"Now he who keeps His commandments abides in Him."
- 1 John 4:7—"Beloved, let us love one another, for love is of God; and everyone who loves is born of God and knows God."
- 1 John 4:8—"He who does not love does not know God, for God is love."
- 1 John 4:9—"In this the love of God was manifested towards us."
- 1 John 4:10—"He loved us and sent His Son."
- 1 John 4:11—"If God so loved us, we also ought to love one another."
- 1 John 4:12—"If we love one another, God abides in us, and His love has been perfected in us."
- 1 John 4:19—"We love Him because He first loved us."
- 1 John 4:20—"If someone says I love God and hates your brother, he is a liar."
- 1 John 4:21—"He who loves God must love his brother also."

- 1 John 5:2—"We know that we love the children of God when we love God and keep His commandments."
- 1 John 5:3—"This is the love of God that we keep His commandments."

In these five chapters, John provides a recap of all the previous teachings on love. He shows us that loving others is simply evidence of the truth that we love the Lord, and so is our obedience to Him.

That all goes back to the teaching on the cost of following. The real question is never "Would you be willing to pay the cost for following?" The question is simply this: "Peter, do you love Me more than these?" Or in other words, whom do you love?

TAKING THE CHAPTER A BIT FURTHER

1. If God is love and we love because He loves us, why does He need to remind us so many times to love one another?
2. Is there any believer you are struggling to love? What is at the heart of that? What do you need to do about it?
3. Our culture rarely associates love with cost. Explain how the two can be tied together.

Chapter 18

It Will Be Worth it All

When I was a child growing up in my little country church, we used to sing a song by the title of this chapter, "It Will Be Worth it All." The song describes the journey of the believer and how that often the struggles and trials are great and severe. It adds that we are prone to worry and complain. But then as the song goes to the chorus, it reminds us that when we see Him, it will truly be worth it all.

The point of the song that no matter what we face in this life, it is nothing compared to what awaits us. As a matter of fact, we can even learn with the apostles the great joy of suffering for Him and how that suffering was even a blessing from God. Look at a few of the things that they said about paying any kind of price for following Jesus.

1. Acts 5:41—"So they departed from the presence of the council, rejoicing that they were counted worthy to suffer shame for His name."
2. Romans 5:3—"And not only *that,* but we also glory in tribulations, knowing that tribulation produces perseverance."
3. Colossians 1:24—"I now rejoice in my sufferings for you, and fill up in my flesh what is lacking in the afflictions of Christ, for the sake of His body, which is the church."
4. Hebrews 10:34—"I now rejoice in my sufferings for you, and fill up in my flesh what is lacking in the afflictions of Christ, for the sake of His body, which is the church."

5. I Peter 4:13—"but rejoice to the extent that you partake of Christ's sufferings, that when His glory is revealed, you may also be glad with exceeding joy."

Clearly, these men knew that following Jesus requires a huge cost. Yet they said they rejoiced in their sufferings! How is it even possible to say that you rejoice in suffering and count it a privilege to suffer for Him? Suffering is painful!

LET'S BE CLEAR

Sacrificing and suffering are neither fun nor pleasant. There is no easy way to say it. Sacrificing and suffering are not high on anyone's list of wants. As a matter of fact, most of us would rather do whatever we can to avoid such calamity.

We want to live comfortably, not painfully. In fact, we may even inflict some pain on ourselves to avoid a more harmful pain. So we go to the dentist to avoid long-term issues with our teeth. We go through the pain of sore muscles in exercise, or depriving ourselves in diets, in order to avoid the greater pain of long-term health issues. We spend much time doing everything we can to avoid "great" pain. Why would we ever entertain the threat of serious pain or enter into any situation that could produce severe suffering? Could there be a benefit to living a life of cost on this side?

I realize that we don't obey to receive, but it is at least a conversation worth having. What comes out of living such a life for Jesus? Now keep in mind, that even if there were no benefits, it should still be worth it. However, there are not only earthly benefits that come from this cost life living, but there are also benefits to come. Remember: it will be worth it all.

EARTHLY BENEFITS OF LIVING THE COST

There are many earthly benefits, but let's just focus on a few. Suffering for Christ will change us for the good. Man is generally self-centered and proud. We know that Scripture clearly states that God resists the proud and gives grace to the humble (James 4:6, I Peter 5:5). God puts us through the fire to remind us that we still have a way to go to be a better man or woman. Rarely does anyone like the pain. Yet few ever complain about the change pain makes in our lives.

Another earthly benefit is the potential to impact other people. When you look through the tears of your eyes into the heart of another who is experiencing the pain of the cost, there is a connection that few understand. Experiencing the cost yourself enables you to hold the hand of another in deeper ways than those who never have dealt with pain.

One more earthly benefit is that the suffering on this side is a strong reminder to keep our eyes on things above. This world we live in has an uncanny ability to grab our hearts. The world is alluring. The world is a trap. The world is fleeting. James says that our lives are a vapor (James 4:14), and will soon be gone. According to Paul, we are already seated in the Heavenlies (Ephesians 2:6). The problem we often have is that this world is such a great place to live, especially in affluent America. But it's all a mirage. Hold on to the world lightly. It has no eternal value.

These are just a few of the examples of some earthly benefits. Maybe you can begin to list some here as well. We need constant reminders that this is not all there is.

SPIRITUAL BENEFITS OF LIVING THE COST

The spiritual benefits to suffering can be exciting! To know that God loves us can be a blessing enough.

We need to understand that everything that comes into our lives flows through His hands. Nothing can get to us or can be part of our lives without His clear authority. He is Sovereign. That means He is in absolute control over us and has full authority over us. Does that make us just robots? Absolutely not. Since He is the Sovereign One, everything is still under His control. He does not cause all things, nor does He make us do things. Yet the final *results* of all things are His and His alone.

He has a goal for every child of His, namely, that we would be conformed to the image of His Son (Romans 8:28–29). It is sad how some theologians have misunderstood the intent of that passage. Far too many want to wrestle forever with the chosen and foreordained and all the other possibilities. But the intent is clear; it all has one purpose—that we would be like Jesus.

The process that our Lord has designed for us to be conformed to His image seems to run straight through the heart of suffering and pain as we learn to navigate following Jesus. There are two ways we can respond to the pain in our lives. The first way is to respond like Joseph. He faced much hardship, but He grew into the man God could use. He went from being a dreamer to a savior. He went from being a self-centered young boy to a man who saw things through the eyes of the Sovereign One. Listen to his own words in Genesis 50:20: "But as for you, you meant evil against me; *but* God meant it for good, in order to bring it about as it is this day, to save many people alive" (KJV). Study also Genesis 45:1–9 where he states that it was God who sent him to Egypt. He saw through his pain and instead saw the loving hand of God. You can also study Job, who boldly stated in Job 1:21, "Naked I came from my mother's womb, and naked shall I return there. The Lord gave, and the Lord has taken away; blessed be the name of the Lord" (KJV). These and others like them learned to see that God's hand over them was far more important than the comfort or ease of this life.

Paul said it this way. "For our light affliction, which is but for a moment, is working for us a far more exceeding and eternal weight of glory" (2 Cor. 4:17). Now does anyone who has studied the life of Paul think he suffered "light affliction"? The only way Paul could have said this is if he had learned to view life through the eyes of eternity, and not through the pain of earth.

Of course, the other choice is to respond like Naomi. You can read her full story in Ruth. It's not pleasant. She suffered a great deal. Unlike Paul, however, when the pain came into her life, she went to the extreme of even changing her name. Naomi exclaims to her countrymen, "Do not call me Naomi; call me Mara, for the Almighty has dealt very bitterly with me" (Ruth 1:20, ESV). She owned up to her own bitterness. Had she suffered much? Absolutely. And it cost her. She should have been the one whom Boaz married (she was the closest kin), but Ruth got the honor. Instead, she saw her pain far too much and chose bitterness. Unfortunately, she is not alone. The path to Heaven is strewn with many who have allowed the things of this world to detract them from the true passion for Christ.

Listen, my dear friend. The path of following Jesus is not an easy road. He never ever said it would be. But He made it clear it would be worth it. May we live our lives with a clear view of eternity and ask daily that He would use whatever to make us ready for His use and His glory. You will never regret it. It will be worth it all.

TAKING THE CHAPTER A BIT FURTHER

1. Romans 8:18–23 reminds us of the better world ahead. What do you think are some of the reasons God permits suffering on this side with an eternal perspective?
2. 2 Corinthians 4:17 says that what we face on this side could be called "light affliction." What are you facing right now that needs this reminder?

Appendix 1

The Cost of Following Jesus Found in the Gospel Accounts

FOLLOWING IS A LIST of all the mentions of (or implications of) cost in the New Testament, along with a few short notes to help you think through their ramifications.

1. Matt. 4:18–22—The call of the apostles where they were first challenged with the cost
    a. They left all
2. Matt. 5:10–12—Blessed are the persecuted
    a. Certainly suggesting that this will be a cost for some
3. Matt. 5:13–16—You are to be salt and light.
    a. Salt must get out of the salt shaker to be effective.
    b. The call to move out of one's shelter and comfort
4. Matt. 5:44—Bless those who persecute you
    a. This is His first major discourse and He has mentioned persecution twice already
5. Matt. 6:20–21—Letting go of treasures on the earth
    a. Choosing to dismiss the treasures of this life

6. Matt. 6:24—Can't serve two masters
    a. Must submit to God
    b. We all serve someone—there is cost when we serve God
7. Matt. 6:33—Seek Him first
    a. This will cost you
8. Matt. 7:13–14—Narrow is the way and gate
    a. Narrow means less options, less freedom, fewer variations
9. Matt. 8:18–22—Follow Me and let go of the rest
    a. So people came to follow Him
    b. His response: it will cost you
10. Matt. 9:9—Call of Matthew
    a. Left his money
    b. Walked away from a lucrative life to follow—cost
11. Matt. 9:38—Harvesting is costly
    a. Jesus says that going out to serve Him is being a laborer in the harvest
    b. He calls it labor, hard work—cost
12. Matt. 10:1ff—Going will cost you
    a. 10:1—the call to go
    b. 10:5ff—not a pretty list if you desire comfort and ease
13. Matt. 10:34–38—The whole passage is about cost
    a. Verse 34—sword
    b. Verse 35–36—foes in his own house
    c. Verse 38—often repeated phrase—take up your cross
    d. Verse 39—lose your life—clearly a cost
14. Matt. 13:21—Tribulation due to the Word
    a. The Word alone can bring on tribulation or persecution
15. Matt. 14:1ff—Cost to John the Baptist
    a. He was the forerunner of Jesus
    b. It cost him his life

16. Matt. 16:24–26—An entire passage on cost
    a. Not unlike Matthew's earlier account in chapter 10
    b. Deny self, take up his cross, lose your life—all sound like cost
17. Matt. 17:21—Prayer and fasting
    a. Ever tried it? Costly
    b. Suggesting a deeper walk will require a price to be paid
18. Matt. 19:21—He taught one man to sell all he had
    a. Obviously this is not true of all, but it was for this man
    b. Why? The danger of riches. We are all so rich in this country
19. Matt. 19:27–30—We have forsaken all
    a. The disciples were merely stating a fact and Jesus certainly did not deny that this was true
20. Matt. 20:26–28—The call to serve
    a. And of course Jesus offers Himself as the example
21. Matt. 22:34–40—a serious call for us to put God and others ahead of self
    a. Love God above all else
    b. The call to love God with all is clear and leaves no room for self love or self elevation—that will cost you
22. Matt. 23:34–35—The pattern of cost
    a. Some of you, not all
    b. But you clearly see the cost of following
23. Matt. 24:4ff—End times cost is coming
    a. Now this is future and more than likely Tribulation, but it is part of following
    b. It is not going to get easier as time goes on
24. Matt. 28:19–20—He promises to be with us because cost is also involved
    a. He knows it is not going to be free of problems
25. Mark 1:16–20—Call to disciples to follow
    a. They forsook their nets (and all that goes with that)
    b. I am not sure we can relate to the price these first followers paid

26. Mark 2:13–14—Call of Matthew
    a. Cost of leaving lucrative lifestyle mentioned earlier
27. Mark 6:7–13—The 12 sent out
    a. He mentions what to do after you are rejected which certainly suggests that they are going to be rejected; hence, probably persecution
28. Mark 6:14—John killed
    a. Potential cost for all of them
    b. They had to know that following Jesus might not have an earthly good ending
29. Mark 8:34—Similar to other passages
    a. Deny self
    b. Take up the cross—must mean the cost of your life
    c. Losing your life—not easy?
30. Mark 9:29—Prayer and fasting
    a. Covered already
    b. Fasting costs us
31. Mark 9:42ff—Even to cut off hand, pluck out eye
    a. Now the full intent of this passage is probably more about salvation
    b. But the idea is be ready to sacrifice if necessary
32. Mark 10:21—One thing you lack
    a. The call and cost
    b. Sometimes it is only one thing, but that one thing can be huge
33. Mark 10:28–31—We have left all
    a. Now again, Jesus does not disagree with them
    b. But notice included in the list of following Him what verse 30 says—with persecutions
34. Mark 10:43–45—Serve
    a. To serve as He served and to give of your life as your Example did
35. Mark 12:41–44—The widow's mite
    a. She gave all even to the point of depriving herself
    b. Jesus commended her sacrifice and used it as a teaching tool for others

36. Mark 13:1ff—End times cost
    a. The future has pain ahead for the followers of Jesus
    b. 13:6, 9, 13: all in His name
37. Luke 5:11—They forsook ALL and followed Him
    a. This was the general sentiment of the followers
38. Luke 5:27—Call of Matthew
    a. Do you think he did not understand the cost when he got up from that table?
    b. Has Jesus' call changed for us today?
39. Luke 6:22—Persecution coming
    a. Notice "when" not "if"
40. Luke 6:40—Be as your Teacher
    a. Would that not include persecution, etc.
    b. Would that imply that following Jesus would not be an easy life
41. Luke 8:13—Times of testing
    a. Again this is questionable whether they are followers or not, but clearly the enemy hates those who even attempt to follow
42. Luke 9:5—They won't receive you
    a. What does that mean?
    b. Can we simply believe it is only verbal resistance?
43. Luke 9:23–26—Numerous places
    a. All writers have these strong statements in their accounts
    b. What does that consistent theme suggest about its importance
44. Luke 9:57–62—No place to lay head
    a. Again, is He our Example?
    b. Does He say we will have similar experiences?
45. Luke 10:3—Sent as lambs to the wolves
    a. Notice verses 10–11
    b. Sounds like a cost to serve
46. Luke 10:27—Love God with all
    a. All leaves no room for making life about self

47. Luke 10:30–37—Parable of the good Samaritan
    a. A story taught by Jesus
    b. Clearly also taught the cost of time, money, and possible ridicule to do what is right. Cost
48. Luke 11:47–49—Previous cost followers paid
    a. There is a history of God's followers who paid a cost to follow
    b. Jesus taught it would continue
49. Luke 12:15—Great points
    a. If it does not consist in what you have, then what does it consist of
    b. Sacrifice and cost?
50. Luke 12:21—Don't lay up for self
    a. The verse before uses the word—fool
    b. To make life about self would be foolish
    c. Not making life about self will cost you
51. Luke 12:32–34—Seek first the Kingdom of God
    a. Again, there is a cost
    b. When we seek Him first
52. Luke 12:53—Family division
    a. Now what will bring this about
    b. You love Jesus more than you love family
53. Luke 13:24—Narrow way
    a. Would not the picture of a narrow way verses a broad way hint that there is a cost
    b. It will not be easy
54. Luke 13:30—To be first, need to be last
    a. Needing to be last means self denial
55. Luke 14:11—Humble self
    a. The obvious challenge—exalt self or humble self
    b. Which costs more?

56. Luke 14:15ff—Excuses for not following
    a. What do the excuses suggest
    b. I want my will over God's will
57. Luke 14:25–33—Deny self
    a. One of Jesus' strongest passages
    b. Given to us by a doctor
58. Luke 16:13—Can't serve 2 masters
    a. Self or God is again the challenge
    b. Which will cost more in this life?
59. Luke 17:9—Servants do what they are called to do
    a. Servants is a major term used of followers—slave
60. Luke 17:33—Lose your life
    a. How many times has Jesus said the same thing
    b. Does losing one's life mean cost?
61. Luke 18:14—Humble self
    a. Pride is much easier and less costly in some ways
    b. Humility will mean dying to self
62. Luke. 18:22—You lack one thing
    a. One thing implies who has rule over your life
    b. The world or Jesus?
63. Luke 18:28–30—Left all
    a. Jesus does not say that they did not leave all?
    b. So, they must have and clearly He is applauding that decision that they made
64. Luke 21:12ff—End times cost
    a. All authors report trouble on the way
    b. It is part of following
65. Luke 22:26–28—Serve and trials
    a. The disciples were arguing about who was the greatest
    b. Jesus calls them to serve and it will cost them

66. John 6:60–66—Some walked away because of the cost
    a. They understood it would cost them to follow
67. John 12:25–26—Hate his life
    a. Hate one's life means putting it last
    b. He connects that with properly serving God
68. John 13:12–17—Serving
    a. What would this look like today?
    b. Serving, cost—put self last
69. John 13:34–35—Love one another at a cost
    a. And it will cost you
    b. Have you ever tried to love the unlovely?
70. John 15:13—Lay down one's life
    a. Put self last and not important
    b. That will cost you the things of this world
71. John 15:19–20—World will hate you
    a. Hate often incurs actions
72. John 17:16—Call to come out of this world
    a. We are called not to be of this world
    b. What does that look like as we follow Jesus?
73. John 21:19ff—Do you love Me more than these
    a. A question we all must ask
    b. Is there anything we love more than Jesus
    c. Our actions prove that answer

Appendix 2

The Cost of Following Jesus Found in the Book of Acts

Some of these are simply statements about what Jesus suffered. Remember that this would have been fresh on the disciple's minds.

1. 1:3—After His passion (suffering and death)
2. 1:13–14—The suffering and death of Jesus undoubtedly was on their minds
3. 2:13—They were mocked
4. 2:23—Jesus was crucified and slain
5. 2:24—The pains of death which we will all face
6. 2:27—The death Jesus experienced
7. 2:43—And fear came upon them
8. 3:13—Jesus was delivered up
9. 3:15—They killed the Prince of Life
10. 3:18—That Christ should suffer
11. 4:3—Peter and John put in prison
12. 4:10—Jesus, whom ye crucified
13. 4:17—Threatened them (cp. 4:21) to not speak of Jesus
14. 4:29—Behold their threatenings

15. 5:11—Fear came upon all the church over the death of Ananias and Sapphira
16. 5:17—Indignation against Peter and John
17. 5:18—Peter and John in prison again
18. 5:28—Commanded not to teach about Jesus
19. 5:30—They slew Jesus and hanged Him on a tree
20. 5:33—They took counsel to slay Peter and the apostles
21. 5:40—They beat the apostles
22. 6:11—Had false witnesses against the apostles
23. 6:12—They came upon Stephen and caught him
24. 6:13–14—They lied against him
25. 7:52—They had persecuted the prophets and were betrayers and murderers of Jesus
26. 7:54—They gnashed at Stephen
27. 7:58—They stoned Stephen
28. 8:1—Great persecution and they had to scatter
29. 8:3—Saul made havoc of the church
30. 8:32–33—Took Jesus' life
31. 9:1—Threatenings and slaughterings against the church
32. 9:2—Believers taken bound
33. 9:13—Evil done to the saints
34. 9:16—Paul told how many great things he must suffer
35. 9:21—Said that Paul had destroyed believers
36. 9:23—Jews took counsel to kill Paul
37. 9:24—Lying in wait to kill him
38. 9:29—They went about to slay Paul
39. 10:39—They slew and hanged Jesus
40. 11:19—The church was persecuted
41. 12:1—Herod wanted to vex the church
42. 12:2—Herod killed James the apostle
43. 12:3—Wanted to kill Peter also

44. 12:4—Put Peter in prison
45. 12:6—He was chained in prison to soldiers
46. 13:8—Elymas tried to turn away some from Jesus
47. 13:28–29—Desired Pilate to kill Jesus
48. 13:45—Spoke against Paul
49. 13:50—Jews stirred up people to persecute Paul and Barnabas
50. 14:2—Stirred up again against the believers
51. 14:5—Wanting to stone Paul and Barnabas
52. 14:6—They were forced to flee
53. 14:19—Paul is stoned and I suspect actually died
54. 14:22—God's people must face tribulation
55. 15:26—Men have hazarded their lives for the name of our Lord Jesus Christ
56. 16:19—Paul and Silas were caught and dragged out
57. 16:21—They were lied about
58. 16:22—They ripped off their clothes and beat them
59. 16:23—Laid many stripes on them
60. 16:24—Put them in stocks
61. 16:39—Chased out of the city
62. 17:3—Christ suffered
63. 17:5—Jews moved with envy and assaulted Jason
64. 17:10—Paul had to flee
65. 18:6—More opposition
66. 18:12—They made insurrection against Paul and brought him to judgment
67. 18:13—They lied about him
68. 18:17—Sosthenes beaten
69. 19:9—They spoke evil of the way (Christians)
70. 19:23—They stirred up others
71. 19:28—Full of wrath against them
72. 19:29—They took Gaius and Aristarchus

73. 20:3—Jews laid in wait for Paul
74. 20:19—Lying in wait again
75. 20:23—Bonds and afflictions were coming for Paul
76. 20:24—Paul counted not his life dear to him
77. 20:29—Grievous wolves after the church
78. 20:30—Speaking perverse things to draw believers away
79. 21:11—Prediction that Paul would be bound
80. 21:13—Paul was ready to die for Christ
81. 21:27—Paul was arrested
82. 21:28—They lied about him
83. 21:30—They took Paul
84. 21:31—Were about to kill him
85. 21:32—They beat him
86. 21:33—Bound with 2 chains
87. 21:36—People wanted to kill him
88. 22:4–5—Paul was once a persecutor of believers
89. 22:19—Paul imprisoned and beat believers
90. 22:20—The blood of the martyr Stephen
91. 22:24—They wanted to scourge Paul
92. 22:25—He was bound again
93. 23:2—They smote him on the mouth
94. 23:10—Paul feared he would be pulled in pieces
95. 23:12—Jews banded together to kill Paul
96. 23:13—40 banded to kill him
97. 23:14—They would not eat until they killed him
98. 23:15—They were ready to kill him
99. 24:2—False accusations against Paul
100. 24:5—Same
101. 24:6—Same
102. 24:23—Solitary confinement
103. 24:27—2 years Paul was bound

104. 25:3—They lay in wait to kill him
105. 25:7—More false accusations
106. 26:10–11—Paul was a persecutor
107. 26:23—Christ suffered
108. 26:69—Bonds
109. 27:1—Sent as a prisoner
110. 27:42—Almost killed
111. 28:16—Paul in solitude with a soldier, two years in prison

Appendix 3

The Cost of Following Jesus Found in the Epistles

1. Romans 1:1
    a. A bondservant
    b. We will see that all the writers used this title for themselves
    c. Basically, a slave—paying the price for following
2. Romans 5:3–4
    a. We glory in tribulations
    b. Tribulations that come from following Christ
3. Romans 8:18
    a. Suffering not worthy to be compared to wait awaits us
    b. Must be in reference to the price we pay for following
4. Romans 8:35–39
    a. Persecution shall not separate us from God
    b. Persecution which comes from following God
5. Romans 12:1–2
    a. Presenting our bodies a living sacrifice
    b. Sacrifice implies cost

6. Romans 12:14–21
   a. Bless those who persecute you
   b. Persecution that come when we follow Him
7. Romans 14:7–8
   a. If we live or die, we do so to the Lord
   b. Certainly not talking about just death in general, but death because we are paying a price
8. Romans 15:3
   a. Christ did not please Himself
   b. Dying to self implies a cost
9. Romans 15:31
   a. Delivered from those who do not believe
   b. Why do we need to be delivered?
10. Romans 16:4
    a. Who risked their lives
    b. Willing to pay the price
11. 1 Corinthians 2:2–3
    a. Paul talks of his fear and trembling
    b. When? As he paid the cost
12. I Corinthians 3:23
    a. We belong to Christ
    b. We are not our own
13. I Corinthians 4:9
    a. We were condemned to death
    b. Compare 1:9 and 4:11
14. I Corinthians 4:11–16
    a. Paul lists the cost of following
    b. Then he says in verse 16 "Imitate me" (as he imitated Christ)
15. I Corinthians 6:19–20
    a. Bought with a price
    b. We are not our own

16. I Corinthians 7:23
    a. Again, bought with a price
    b. How many times does Paul need to tell us
17. I Corinthians 8:6
    a. We are for Him
    b. Meaning: not for ourselves
18. I Corinthians 11:1
    a. Imitate me as I imitate Christ
    b. Would that not include suffering?
19. I Corinthians 16:9
    a. There are many adversaries
    b. Because we follow Christ
20. 2 Corinthians 1:3–7
    a. Tribulations, sufferings of Christ, partakers of His sufferings
    b. All because we follow Christ
21. 2 Corinthians 1:9
    a. Sentence of death on us
    b. Compare 4:9,11
22. 2 Corinthians 4:5
    a. Use of bondservants again
    b. Not just in the introduction
23. 2 Corinthians 4:8–15
    a. Pressed, persecuted, dying of the Lord, delivered to death
    b. He saw his life as not his own and fragile
24. 2 Corinthians 4:16–18
    a. This light affliction
    b. That was Paul's perspective on suffering for Jesus
25. 2 Corinthians 6:4–5
    a. Stripes, prisons, etc.
    b. All part of the cost

26. 2 Corinthians 7:3
    a. To die and live with you
    b. Paul realized he may lose his life to follow
27. 2 Corinthians 7:5
    a. Troubled on every side
    b. Troubled by what? And for what?
28. 2 Corinthians 8:2
    a. Great trial of affliction
    b. Paying the price
29. 2 Corinthians 11:23–28
    a. All for following Jesus
    b. Quite a list
30. 2 Corinthians 12:1–5
    a. This is probably the example of Paul actually being killed in Acts 14:19–20
    b. Killed for his faith
31. 2 Corinthians 12:10
    a. Persecution for Christ's sake
    b. The cost
32. Galatians 2:20
    a. Crucified with Christ
    b. Does that not imply what Jesus taught about carrying our cross
33. Galatians 6:12–14
    a. Suffering for cross of Christ
    b. Cost involved?
34. Ephesians 4:1
    a. A prisoner of the Lord
    b. Not just physical
35. Ephesians 5:1–2
    a. Imitate God and be an offering/sacrifice
    b. Cost clearly implied

36. Philippians 1:12–14
    a. Chains in Christ
    b. Because he is a follower
37. Philippians 1:21
    a. For me to live is Christ
    b. To die for Christ also cost
38. Philippians 1:29
    a. Believe and suffer
    b. We seem to accept the "believe" but why not the suffering as also our call?
39. Colossians 1:24
    a. Rejoice in sufferings and afflictions of Christ
    b. Paying the price for following
40. Colossians 2:20
    a. Died with Christ
    b. Clear theme that this life is not our own
41. Colossians 3:1–4
    a. We are dead
    b. It is what happens when we follow
42. Colossians 4:10
    a. A fellow prisoner
    b. In prison because he follows Christ
43. I Thessalonians 1:6–7
    a. Received the Word in much affliction
    b. Cost for even receiving the Word
44. I Thessalonians 2:2
    a. Suffered at Philippi?
    b. Why? For the Gospel
45. I Thessalonians 2:14–15
    a. Suffering, persecution
    b. For following Jesus

46. I Thessalonians 3:3–4
    a. We told you it was coming
    b. Following Jesus is costly
47. 2 Thessalonians 1:4–6
    a. Persecution
    b. Why? Following Jesus
48. I Timothy 4:10
    a. Suffer reproach
    b. For the cause of Christ
49. 2 Timothy 3:10–12
    a. All who live Godly will suffer persecution
    b. Seems like it is certain to happen
50. 2 Timothy 4:6–7
    a. Poured out as a drink offering
    b. Suffered and now about to die for the cause
51. 2 Timothy 4:17
    a. Out of the mouth of the lion
    b. Whoever that is, does it not sound like cost?
52. Titus 1:1
    a. Bondservant
    b. My life is not my own
53. Philemon 1
    a. Bondservant
    b. Again, the cost
54. Hebrews 2:9
    a. Suffering of death
    b. The example that Jesus left for us
55. Hebrews 5:8
    a. Things He suffered
    b. Again, He laid out the cost

56. Hebrews 10:34
    a. Chains
    b. Paying the price
57. Hebrews 11
    a. The whole chapter in some ways
    b. But particularly 11:32–38—of whom the world was not worthy
58. Hebrews 12:2
    a. Endured the cross
    b. Again, left us an example
59. Hebrews 13:3
    a. Bonds, suffering adversity
    b. Why? For being a follower
60. James 1:2–5
    a. Trials
    b. Do we believe James was concerned about the silly trials of life or the ones connected with the cost of following Jesus
61. James 5:10
    a. Prophets are an example of suffering
    b. Again, more examples of the cost even in the Old Testament
62. I Peter 1:6–7
    a. Trials
    b. Again, see comments on James 1:2–5
63. I Peter 1:11
    a. Suffering of Christ
    b. Our Example
64. I Peter 2:18–23
    a. Do good and suffer for it
    b. For this you were called
65. I Peter 3:9
    a. You were called to this
    b. Would that not include the pain of this verse?

66. I Peter 3:14, 17–18
    a. Suffering, Christ suffered
    b. His Example is clearly our example to follow
67. I Peter 4:1
    a. Arm yourself with the same mind
    b. What mind? Christ's sufferings
68. I Peter 4:12–19
    a. Partakers of Christ's sufferings
    b. Clearly for following
69. I Peter 5:8
    a. Roaring lion
    b. Why does he want to devour us?
70. I Peter 5:10
    a. After you have suffered a while
    b. It is part of following
71. 2 Peter 1:1
    a. A bondservant
    b. Peter uses the same title as Paul and others
72. I John 2:6
    a. Walk as Jesus
    b. Would that not imply all He faced?
73. I John 2:15–17
    a. Love not the world
    b. Why? Because we are not called to be of this world.
74. I John 3:16
    a. To lay down our lives
    b. Cost for sure
75. (2 & 3 John do not seem to have examples)
76. Jude 1
    a. Again, bondservant
    b. The title of all the authors: slave

77. Revelation 2:10

a. Do not fear what you are about to suffer

b. Suffering for the cause of Christ?

78. Revelation 2:13

a. Antipas, My faithful martyr

b. Gave his life for Christ

Appendix 4

The "One Anothers" In the New Testament

1. Mark 9:50
    a. Have peace one with another
    b. The phrase is a present active imperative
    c. The context is about relationships
    d. Salt is about seasoning one another
    e. His thought here is clearly body life
2. John 13:14
    a. This is not an exact imperative and therefore is not to be taken literally that we need to take the shoes off of our neighbor and wash his/her feet
    b. The idea is from the thought of this passage—serve one another
    c. Jesus is challenging the disciples to meet the needs of one another.
    d. Question: how can you do this if you don't spend time and connect with others?
3. John 13:34
    a. This is the dominant one in the NT, found 15 times
    b. And to put that in perspective, the closest second only occurs four times

c. Jesus clearly introduced it as a command—a new commandment I give unto you

d. Paul, John, and Peter add this one in their writings

e. We ought to love one another

f. Does that just mean when we come across a need?

g. Does that just mean when we feel like it?

h. Does it imply an active attempt to live out this love. In other words, should we be attempting to make sure we are fulfilling this for one another?

i. It should be an active part of who we are

4. Romans 12:5

a. Members of one another

b. This suggests true body life and connection

c. We are part of one another

d. Ephesians 4:25 says the same and is in the context of relationships with one another

e. This will involve spending time with one another

5. Romans 12:10a

a. Be kindly affectionate to one another

b. In other words, our lives ought to be characterized by someone who acts out care, concern, affection

6. Romans 12:10b

a. In honor giving preference to one another

b. The idea is to go before, lead or set the example

c. In other words: I value you more important than me

d. How are you doing that in the body?

e. Are you just doing so for your select buddies?

7. Romans 12:16

a. Be of the same mind toward one another

b. Let your mind dwell on these things

c. This suggests contemplative action—working at bringing thoughts into captivity to this meaning

   d. I will choose to have thoughts towards you—I will think on you
   e. And from the NT, we know that means good thoughts
8. Romans 14:19
   a. Edify one another
   b. The idea is to "build up one another"
   c. That is so contrary to the way of the world times
   d. Jesus clearly introduced it as a command—a new commandment I give unto you
   e. Paul, John, and Peter all add this one in their writings
   f. We ought to love one another
   g. Does that just mean when we come across a need?
   h. Does that just mean when we feel like it?
   i. Does it imply an active attempt to live out this love?
   j. In other words, should we be attempting to make sure we are fulfilling this for one another?
9. Romans 15:7
   a. Receive one another
   b. Receive suggests hospitality
   c. Receive suggests actively reaching out to others
   d. Receive suggests getting out of your comfort zone
10. Romans 15:14
   a. Admonish one another
      i. This might suggest more than just a gentle rebuke
      ii. It might be a warning to a brother or sister
      iii. Many of us never get that close to be able to do so, yet we are told to do so
      iv. Living life at a distance from your church family prevents you from knowing how to help those in your family

11. Romans 16:16
    a. Salute one another
        i. This one actually occurs four times in the NT
        ii. Not sure exactly what it means, but it does appear to suggest relationships
12. I Corinthians 11:33
    a. Tarry for one another
        i. This was a command connected to the love feasts in the NT where the believers came together for food
        ii. Some jumped right in and never waited for those who were not there yet
        iii. It was an act of insensitivity to the body
13. I Corinthians 12:25
    a. Have the same care for one another
    b. And the next verse gives us the details
    c. How can you do this if you are not spending time together?
14. Galatians 5:13
    a. Through love, serve one another
    b. Verse 14 adds the importance of loving your neighbor
    c. Serve again involves relationships, connecting, etc.
15. Galatians 6:2
    a. Bear one another's burdens
    b. How many burdens are you bearing for your brothers and sistersIs it possible that you are so disconnected with your own life that you have lost the passion for others in your family?
16. Ephesians 4:2
    a. Forbearing with one another
    b. Basically put: putting up with one another
    c. Today, we have on patience with anyone but ourselves, and that is growing thin
    d. Same idea in Colossians 3:13—forbear and forgive

17. Ephesians 4:32
    a. Be kind to one another
    b. Again, it is a command
    c. Do you think it just means when you come in contact
    d. Is this the only time, or should we be caring for each other in such a way that our kindness is a natural outgrowth of who we are?
18. Ephesians 5:21
    a. Submit to one another
    b. Again, putting the other person first
    c. That must mean we are in close contact with one another
19. Philippians 2:3
    a. Esteem one another better than self
    b. The heart of this is true humility
    c. Esteem here suggests that it is an act that is lead before the mind—or, an active mind focusing on how to do it
    d. Premeditated esteeming others better
    e. Looking for opportunities—that means you are with one another
20. I Thessalonians 4:18
    a. Comfort one another
    b. How can you do this apart from one another?
21. I Thessalonians 5:15
    a. Pursue good unto one another
    b. Again, the idea includes putting some thought into this
    c. How can I do good for that brother or sister?
22. Hebrews 10:24
    a. Consider one another
    b. Put this in your mind
23. James 5:16
    a. Confess your sins to one another
    b. That must involve relationships

24. James 5:16

    a. Pray on behalf of one another

    b. Certainly this means specific prayers! So and so is sick, such and such needs monetary help, etc.

25. I Peter 4:7

    a. Be hospitable to one another

    b. Use the home that God gave you for others

    c. It is amazing how some folks never have anyone in their home

    d. What do you think that home is for?

26. And there are 5 more of a negative nature

    a. Let us not judge one another—Romans 14:13

    b. Don't defraud one another—I Cor. 7:5

    c. Lie not to one another—Col. 3:9

    d. Don't speak against one another—James 4:11

    e. Do not murmur against one another—James 5:9

Bibliography

Grant, George. "A History of Persecution." *Tabletalk Magazine*, 1 August 2015.

Martin, Cath. "70 Million Christians Martyred for their Faith Since Jesus Walked on the Earth." *Christian Today*, 25 June 2014.

Redmayne, Eddie, and Aaron Tviet. "ABC Cafe / Red and Black." *Les Miserables: The Motion Picture Soundtrack*. 2012.

Robinson, Robert Clifton. "Six Illegal Trials." 10 May 2014. https://robertcliftonrobinson.com/tag/six-illegal-trials/.

Swindoll, Charles. *Hope Again: When Life Hurts and Dreams Fade*. Nashville: Nelson, 1997.

Taylor, Mike. "The Jealousy of God." 16 January 2004. http://www.miketaylor.org.uk/xian/jealous.html

Thoennes, K. Erik. *Godly Jealousy: A Theology of Intolerant Love*. Scotland: Christian Focus, 2005.

Walker, Peter. "900,000 Christians Were 'Martyred' Over Last Decade, Says Christian Research." *Independent*, 13 January 2017.

CPSIA information can be obtained
at www.ICGtesting.com
Printed in the USA
BVHW071037210721
612427BV00018B/956

9 781666 704815